THREE ZEN MASTERS

THREE ZEN MASTERS

IKKYŪ, HAKUIN, AND RYŌKAN

John Stevens

KODANSHA INTERNATIONAL
Tokyo, New York, London

Distributed in the United States by Kodansha America, Inc., 114 Fifth Avenue, New York, N.Y. 10011, and in the United Kingdom and continental Europe by Kodansha Europe Ltd., Gillingham House, 38–44 Gillingham Street, London SW1V 1HU. Published by Kodansha International Ltd., 17-14 Otowa 1-chome, Bunkyo-ku, Tokyo 112, and Kodansha America Inc. Edited by Optima Co., Ltd.
First edition, 1993

93 94 95 5 4 3 2 1
ISBN 4-7700-1651-4

Contents

PREFACE

Three Zen Masters tells the life stories of Ikkyū Sōjun (1394–1481), Hakuin Ekaku (1686–1768), and Ryōkan Taigu (1758–1831). Each one manifested Zen in his own way. Radical Ikkyū, the "Crazy Cloud," was unconventional, uncompromising, and combative. He relentlessly attacked sham and hypocrisy, concealing nothing himself, even his sex life, which makes him unique among stony-faced Zen priests, who usually mask their emotions so well.

While Ikkyū denounced the diploma system of the Zen establishment, rejecting an *inka*, or "certificate of enlightenment," from his master and refusing to present such documents to his own disciples, Hakuin passed out more diplomas than any other bona fide master in Japanese history, using the system to cultivate a small army of Zen practitioners who strove to see into their natures and become Buddhas. Big, bold, and dynamic, Hakuin insisted that everyone—male or female, monastic or lay, peasant or lord—could practice "meditation in action."

Ryōkan, in contrast, was a gentle, reclusive, and self-effacing Zen master. Never an abbot, Ryōkan lived quietly and simply in little hermitages, passing his days playing with village children, drinking saké with local farmers, communing with nature, and writing poems.

All three masters were artists of the highest order, employing brush, ink, and paper as a means to transmit Zen teachings.

Over the centuries, the magnificent artwork of Ikkyū, Hakuin, and Ryōkan—brushstrokes of enlightenment—has inspired, instructed, and delighted generations of Zen students.

Although I have relied principally on primary sources for the biographical material on Ikkyū, I considered it necessary to include a number of the most plausible anecdotes told about this singular monk in order to portray the image of Ikkyū that is cherished by his many admirers. And even if not literally true, each story conveys an important Zen message characteristic of Ikkyū. Regarding the lives of Hakuin and Ryōkan, we are on much surer ground, thanks to the abundance of autobiographical material and contemporary accounts available for these two masters. All of the translations appearing here are my own.

Zen is particular and universal. The particulars of *Three Zen Masters* relate to time, place, and circumstance; the universal is the essence of Zen revealed in the lives and teachings of Ikkyū, Hakuin, and Ryōkan. Together they present a timeless message that can be appreciated by everyone in any era.

JOHN STEVENS
Honolulu, 1992

IKKYŪ SŌJUN
(1394–1481)

IKKYŪ was born at sunrise on the first day of 1394. Although rumored to be the son of the young emperor Go-Komatsu (1377–1433), at birth Ikkyū was registered as a commoner. His mother, a lady-in-waiting at the court and a favorite of Go-Komatsu, had been unjustly ousted from the palace by the machinations of the jealous empress and her supporters. Consequently, the circumstances surrounding Ikkyū's birth were humble, although his earliest biography states that even as an infant he "bore the signs of a dragon and the marks of a phoenix."

At the age of five, Ikkyū was sent to be an acolyte at Ankoku-ji, a Zen temple in Kyoto. There he would be assured of a good education, as well as protection from scheming court officials and suspicious generals. This was important in medieval Japan since even the bastard son of the emperor—given the right circumstances and powerful backers—could claim the throne. At Ankoku-ji, Ikkyū was drilled in Buddhist scriptures and the classics of China and Japan. A brilliant student whose genius was recognized by all, Ikkyū was also a quick-witted and mischievous child. Here are a few anecdotes from his days as a precocious acolyte.

Not long after entering the temple, the abbot ordered Ikkyū to extinguish the candles on the altar before turning in for the night. When Ikkyū returned to pronounce the act done, the abbot asked, "By the way, how did you put the candles out?"

"By blowing," Ikkyū replied.

"Never do that," the abbot scolded him. "The Buddha is holy and human breath is dirty. Extinguish the flames by waving your hand or using a fan."

The following morning, when the abbot entered the main hall for the morning service, he noticed Ikkyū chanting away with his back to the altar.

"What are you doing, you little fool!" the abbot exploded.

"You told me that human breath was dirty and should not be directed toward images of the Buddha. How can we chant without breathing?"

"This is different," the nonplussed abbot mumbled, and he ordered Ikkyū to turn around.

Ikkyū, though, was irrepressible. The abbot was very fond of a certain candy and kept the treasured sweet in a jar in his room, warning Ikkyū and the other temple boys, "This candy is beneficial for grown-ups, but if a child eats it he will die immediately."

Ikkyū was not fooled for a second, and as soon as the abbot was away he emptied the jar and shared the contents with his friends. Ikkyū then broke one of the tea bowls in the abbot's room. When the abbot returned he found Ikkyū in tears.

"While cleaning your honored room," Ikkyū sobbed convincingly, "I accidently broke this precious bowl. To make amends for my terrible misdeed, I swallowed some of the poisoned candy. Nothing happened so I took all of it, sure that it would finish me off as you said it would. I didn't die, unfortunately, so please forgive me."

Another time, one of the other acolytes accidently broke the abbot's favorite tea bowl while cleaning his quarters. Terrified of the abbot's fury, the acolyte pleaded with the resourceful Ikkyū to get him out of the jam. "Leave it to me," Ikkyū reassured him. When the abbot returned to the temple, Ikkyū met him at the entrance hall.

"Master," Ikkyū said softly, "you have often taught us that

everything that is born must die, and whatever possesses material form will eventually perish."

"Yes," the abbot responded. "Those are the inescapable realities of life."

"Master, I have bad news for you," Ikkyū said sadly. "It was time for your favorite tea bowl to die."

The smart little monk's reputation reached the ears of Shogun Yoshimitsu (1358–1408), and Ikkyū was summoned to the castle for a meeting.

"I've heard that you are quite bright," the shogun said to Ikkyū. "Do you think you can catch a tiger?"

"Yes, my lord, I believe I can," Ikkyū replied with great confidence.

"Here is a rope. Catch that one," the shogun challenged, pointing to a tiger painted on a large screen in the room.

Without hesitation, Ikkyū placed himself in front of the screen, readied the rope, and shouted, "Now, my lord, please drive the tiger out!"

A certain patron of the temple was fond of leather clothing, which is not considered appropriate garb by Buddhists. One day, as he approached the temple, he was greeted with a sign on a board that read, "Leather goods are not allowed on temple grounds. Those who break this rule will be severely beaten." Recognizing the calligraphy to be that of the impish Ikkyū, the patron stormed in, furious with the child monk.

"What about the big drum in the main hall?" the patron demanded to know. "Isn't that covered with leather?"

"Yes, that's true," replied Ikkyū. "But then we beat it soundly morning and evening. If you insist on wearing leather, you will get the same treatment."

In an attempt to turn the tables on Ikkyū, the patron invited the abbot and Ikkyū to a feast of vegetarian dishes. In Ikkyū's bowl, however, there was a mound of fish. Ikkyū promptly gobbled it up.

"Just a minute," the patron chided Ikkyū. "Don't you know that Buddhist monks are not allowed to eat flesh?"

"My mouth is like the Kamakura Highway," Ikkyū informed him. "High things and low, butchers and greengrocers, all travel down it unimpeded."

Determined to get the better of the smart aleck, the patron whipped out his sword.

"How will this go down?" he asked menacingly.

"Friend or foe?" Ikkyū inquired.

"Foe!" the patron yelled.

"Enemies cannot pass!" Ikkyū said defiantly.

"Friend, then!" the patron exclaimed.

Ikkyū coughed as if choking. "Sorry, the gate has just closed."

In a similar tale, the long-suffering abbot was caught eating fish soup by Ikkyū.

"Master, you've stated that flesh was absolutely forbidden as food in this temple. But if it is all right now," Ikkyū said, eyeing the bowl, "then I'd like some, too."

"No, no," the abbot insisted. "It is indeed a great sin for novices to eat flesh. In my case, however, I am actually conducting a funeral service for the fish."

"How's that?" Ikkyū wanted to know.

"I said to it, 'Fish, you are now like a withered branch. Even if I let you go, you can never return to the water. If I take you as medicine, however, you may attain Buddhahood soon!'"

The next day Ikkyū hightailed it over to the fish market and bought a live carp. Just as he was about to chop it up, the abbot walked in.

"What are you doing! Killing a living thing is ten times worse than eating one!" he exclaimed.

"No, no, listen to this," Ikkyū told the abbot as he picked up the wriggling fish. "Fish, you are like a living branch. If I let you go, you will escape and I'll go hungry. Rather than you swimming around in the water, let me enjoy you for dinner."

So saying, he lopped off the fish's head and put it in his soup.

His hypocrisy exposed once again, the exasperated abbot was speechless. Such shock tactics became Ikkyū's trademark.

Ikkyū composed his first formal Chinese-style poem, a particularly demanding art form, when he was just twelve years of age.

> "*Withered Grasses near the Manor*"
> In the desolation of autumn, an abandoned beauty
>   sings.
> No messengers come to summon her back to the
>   manor.
> Glory and disgrace, joy and sorrow—she has
>   seen it all.
> Her lord's favor was shallow, but the grasses of
>   neglect are deep.

As a child Ikkyū may have been full of playfulness, but there was always a serious side to his character. This poem is permeated with Buddhist pessimism, a lament on the impermanence of things, and it reflects Ikkyū's deep resentment at the manner in which his mother had been treated. Ikkyū seems to have been particularly close to his mother, and he never overcame his bitterness regarding her undeserved banishment from the court. In another poem composed later in his life, Ikkyū frets:

> Such a refined beauty, rouged and powdered,
> Even the Buddha could not resist her;
> She possesses the soul of China's Jade Beauty
> Yet it is in Japan that she now languishes.

In addition to decrying the unjust treatment of his mother, these two poems reveal a further preoccupation of Ikkyū: the often troubled relationship between men and women. Given the degeneracy of the times, Ikkyū likely received an early initiation into homosexual love at his temple. Ikkyū lost interest in that type of love, but his fascination with the opposite sex would remain to the very last day of his eighty-seven years.

In 1410, appalled by the greed and corruption of the senior

monks, the sixteen-year-old Ikkyū fled Ankoku-ji. He announced his departure with this poem:

> Filled with shame, I can barely hold my tongue.
> Zen words are overwhelmed and demonic forces
>   emerge victorious.
> These monks are supposed to lecture on Zen,
> But all they do is boast of family history.

Ikkyū went to train under Ken'ō (d. 1414), an eccentric old monk who lived in a secluded, tumbledown hut in the hills outside Kyoto. Earlier in his life Ken'ō had caused a stir when he refused to accept an *inka*, a certificate of enlightenment, from Muin, then abbot of Myōshin-ji. In those days such certificates—often purchased or fraudulently obtained—were essential for winning a position at a major temple. Thus, Ken'ō's act of rebellion excluded him from becoming a member of the Zen establishment—which suited him and his single disciple, the stubborn and determined Ikkyū, just fine.

At the same time Ikkyū also studied literature with a scholar-monk named Seisō. One day, Shogun Yoshimochi (1386–1428) appeared at the entrance hall of Seisō's temple and demanded to examine a certain scroll that was in the temple's possession. While the other students cowered in the corner, Ikkyū boldly brought out the scroll, but would not step down into the entrance hall to give it to the shogun or his aide as etiquette demanded. Finally, the shogun, who had had run-ins with Ikkyū before, came forward to take the scroll himself. After giving it a glance, the shogun returned the scroll, then left without further comment. The young Ikkyū was subsequently praised for his courage in standing up to the overbearing civil authorities.

Ikkyū remained with Ken'ō until that uncompromising monk's death in 1414. After serving as his master's gravedigger and sole mourner, the distraught Ikkyū wandered aimlessly around Kyoto, lamenting his loss and trying to assuage the pain with chanting and meditation. He visited his mother several times during this bleak period, and she was so concerned about his disheveled appearance and confused state of mind that she surreptitiously assigned a servant to follow her son on his wanderings.

Totally despondent, Ikkyū resolved to throw himself into Lake Biwa, saying, "If I am useless here on earth, at least let me be good fish-food!" Fortunately, his mother's servant was nearby and put a stop to Ikkyū's suicide. After Ikkyū calmed down, the servant handed him a letter from his mother in which she pleaded with him to remain alive for her sake. She also wrote: "Enlightenment will be yours someday; please persevere." Ikkyū agreed to return to his mother's home and ponder his fate further.

He decided to seek acceptance as a disciple of Kasō (1352–1428), who was a master considered even more severe than Ken'ō. Those two harsh taskmasters well represented the demanding Daitō tradition of Zen. Daitō (Shūhō Myōchō, 1282–1337), after gaining enlightenment under Daiō (Nanpō Jomyō, 1235–1308), had spent some years deepening his realization while living as a beggar in the vicinity of Kyoto's Fifth Avenue Bridge. Outlaws around the bridge liked to test the temper of their blades on the helpless beggars there, but when the bandits threatened Daitō one night, he faced them with unflinching calm.

> My trials continue
> On and on—
> Now I'll see
> How steady
> My mind really is.

Disarmed by Daitō's unshakable presence of mind, the ruffians thereafter left him alone.

Even after Emperor Hanazono had installed Daitō as the first abbot of Daitoku-ji in 1324, the monk upheld his harsh discipline, both for his students and himself. To this day, Daitō's "Final Admonitions" are still recited at Daitoku-ji.

All of you who have come to this mountain monastery, do not forget that you are here for the sake of the Way, not for the sake of clothing and food. . . . Address yourselves throughout the day to knowing the unknowable. From start to finish, investigate all things in detail. Time flies like an arrow, so do not waste energy on trivial matters. Be attentive! Be attentive!

After this old monk completes his pilgrimage, some of you may preside over grand temples with magnificent buildings and huge libraries adorned with gold and silver and have many followers. Others may devote themselves to sutra study, esoteric chants, continual meditation, and strict observance of the precepts. Whatever the course of action, if the mind is not set on the marvelous, transcendent Way of the Buddhas and Patriarchs, causality is negated and the teaching collapses. Such people are devils and can never be my true heirs. The one who tends to his own affairs and clarifies his own nature, even though he may be residing in the remote countryside in a hut, subsisting on wild vegetables cooked in a battered old cauldron, encounters my tradition daily and receives my teaching with gratitude. Who can take this lightly? Work harder! Work harder!

On the day of his death, Daitō, who was lame in one leg, addressed his misshapen limb: "All my life I have followed you, but today you are going to follow me!" So saying, he forced the leg into the proper meditation position, breaking the bone, which pierced his skin.

Kasō was also, for a brief period, the abbot of Daitoku-ji, although he much preferred to stay at his small retreat near Lake Biwa. In contrast to the opulence and frivolity of Daitoku-ji, the regimen at Kasō's retreat tested the mettle of even the most earnest of disciples. When Ikkyū presented himself there, he was refused admittance in no uncertain terms. Ikkyū persisted, planting himself at the gate for the next five days until the abuse became physical—the gatekeeper doused him with slops and beat him with a broom. Undeterred, Ikkyū withstood nearly a week of such humiliating punishment before Kasō relented and let him in. As a member of Kasō's community, Ikkyū underwent the entire regime: heavy manual work, meager food, little sleep, and long hours of meditation.

Due to his artistic skill, however, Ikkyū gained some respite from the grueling schedule when he did some work for shops in Kyoto, such as painting dolls using his own kimono designs and making incense sachets. The money he earned helped support Kasō's retreat.

Ikkyū studied various *kōan* under Kasō but was particularly perplexed by this one from the fifteeenth case of the *Gateless Gate* (*Mumonkan*):

> When Tung-shan [910–90] came to study with Yün-men [d. 949], the master asked the monk, "Where are you from?"
>
> "From the Ch'a district," Tung-shan replied.
>
> "Where did you train during the summer?" Yün-men wanted to know.
>
> "At Dao Monastery in Honan."
>
> "When did you leave there?"
>
> "On August twenty-fifth."
>
> "You deserve sixty blows of my stick!" Yünmen thundered [although he did not actually strike him].
>
> The next day Tung-shan returned to Yün-men and asked, "Yesterday you said I deserved sixty blows of your staff. Where am I at fault?"
>
> "You worthless rice bag! Why are you wandering around here and there?"
>
> Tung-shan suddenly attained enlightenment.

One day, when Ikkyū was in town, he heard a blind minstrel recounting the tale of Lady Giō, who was a favorite of the Heian-period general Taira no Kiyomori (d. 1181) but was spurned when the general fell for another beauty, Hotoke ("the Buddha"). In the end, both girls grew weary of the world and its woes and became nuns. For reasons clear only to Ikkyū, when he heard this particular song he grasped the significance of "You deserve sixty blows of my stick!"

Prior to this incident, Ikkyū had been called Shūken, but Kasō was so impressed by the event that he bestowed upon his disciple the Buddhist name "Ikkyū," or "One Pause," signifying the repose between life and death, illusion and enlightenment.

Despite the insight he had achieved, Ikkyū continued to struggle with physical and mental obstacles. He took to meditating throughout the night on Lake Biwa in a boat borrowed from a fisherman. One midsummer night in 1420, as the twenty-six-year-old Ikkyū drifted across the still lake, a crow cawed raucously. In that instant Ikkyū had a profound realization.

When Ikkyū went to tell Kasō, his teacher sneered, "You may be an Arhat, but you are still no master!"

Ikkyū replied nonchalantly, "Being an Arhat is fine with me. Who needs to be a master?"

Kasō was pleased. "Then you really are a master!" he said.

Kasō also demanded an "enlightenment poem," as was the custom, and Ikkyū produced this verse:

Ikkyū's Calligraphy, Reading, "Ikkyū" (One Pause). (Fujita Art Museum, Japan)
The single brushstroke for "one" doubles as a phallic symbol, sex being an essential element of Ikkyū's Zen. The poem above Ikkyū's name laments:

> The brilliance of Daitō is nearly extinguished.
> Nowadays, who at Mount Ryūhō [Daitoku-ji]
>   knows anything about him?
> A thousand years hence, only the descendants of
>   Tōkai [Ikkyū]
> Will struggle to keep his spirit alive.

大燈佛法没光輝

龍寶山中又一誰

東海兒孫千萬億

吟䑓禪詩

For ten years I was in turmoil,
Seething and angry, but now my time has come!
The crow laughs, an Arhat emerges from the
    filth,
And in the sunlight of Chao-yang, a jade beauty
    sings.

The last line, referring to yet another abandoned beauty in ancient China, seems to indicate that the enlightened Ikkyū has finally reconciled himself to his mother's fate.

It is said that when Kasō presented Ikkyū with an *inka* Ikkyū hurled it to the ground in protest and stomped away. Kasō had the *inka* kept safely by one of his leading female disciples in the hope that Ikkyū would someday relent and accept it. Much later, when Ikkyū learned of its existence, he had it brought to him and proceeded to tear the document to pieces. When Ikkyū discovered that his disciples had pieced the *inka* together, he seized the paper and burned it. Despite this, Ikkyū remained with Kasō for several years following his experience of enlightenment. He was so devoted to Kasō that he cleaned up his master's excrement with his bare hands when the ailing Kasō had diarrhea and soiled himself. Nevertheless, the two had a falling-out around 1426, and Ikkyū suddenly left the monastery.

One reason for the discord was Ikkyū's loathing of Yōsō, who was Kasō's other chief disciple. Yōsō was quite a bit senior to Ikkyū but was unlike him in every way, and the two were never able to get along. Another likely cause of Ikkyū's departure was his increasingly unconventional and erratic behavior. Kasō, for example, once remonstrated with Ikkyū for showing up at the memorial service for Kasō's master, Gongai, in ragged robes and broken straw sandals—even the austere Kasō believed that one should dress properly to honor the dead—but Ikkyū just snorted, "I am dressed the way a monk should be. All these other imposters are just decked out in glorified shit-covers!"

After this incident Kasō is reported to have said, "Ikkyū is my true heir, but his ways are mad." At this time Ikkyū also adopted the custom of "spending mornings in the mountains and nights in the town"—practicing monastic Zen during the day and carousing Zen after dark. Eventually, Ikkyū was obliged to leave Kasō's community.

After setting out on his own, Ikkyū reportedly had a meeting with the retired Emperor Go-Komatsu in 1427, which could be interpreted as a reconciliation between father and bastard son. Go-Komatsu solicited and received Ikkyū's counsel on several important secular and religious matters, and thereafter the two apparently met regularly. Ikkyū was summoned to Go-Komatsu's deathbed in 1433 and presented with several paintings and calligraphic works from the imperial collection. Ikkyū, who had "never owned so much as a pin," cherished the precious scrolls to the end of his days.

Kasō died in 1428. His death verse was:

> A drop of water freezes in midair.
> My seventy-seven years
> All used up!
> Spring water bubbles up from the flames.

Ikkyū attended the master's funeral, after which all of Kasō's disciples went their own ways. Ikkyū himself never settled down but passed the rest of his life roaming the Kyoto area, a self-described "Crazy Cloud."

> A crazy cloud, out in the open,
> Blown about madly, as wild as they come!
> Who knows where this cloud will gather, where
>   the wind will settle?
> The sun rises from the eastern sea, and shines
>   over the land.

Early in this period, one of Ikkyū's poems hints he may have taken a common-law wife (and, according some accounts, fathered a child).

> Exhausted with homosexual pleasures, I embrace
>   my wife.
> The narrow path of asceticism is not for me;
> My mind runs in the opposite direction.
> It is easy to be glib about Zen—I'll just keep my
>   mouth shut
> And rely on love-play all day long.

Ikkyū spent a great deal of time in the bustling city of Sakai, where he quickly became a favorite of the prosperous merchants, who were charmed by his antics. He alternated pleasant interludes at the residences of the rich and powerful with long retreats in remote tumbledown hermitages, devoting himself to old-fashioned Zen training.

Due to his popularity, in 1440 Ikkyū was called to serve as abbot of Nyoi-an, a subtemple of Daitoku-ji. However, he quickly grew disgusted with the sham and hypocrisy about him and abruptly announced his resignation with this verse:

> Ten days in this temple and my mind is reeling!
> Between my legs the red thread stretches
>   and stretches.
> If you come some other day asking for me,
> Better look in a fish stall, a saké shop,
>   or a brothel.

The red thread of passion refers to a sex *kōan* first posed by the Chinese master Sung-yüan (Shōgen, d. 1202):

> In order to know the Way in perfect clarity,
> there is one essential point you must penetrate
> and not avoid: the red thread of passion between
> our legs that cannot be severed. Few face up to
> the problem, since it is not at all easy to settle.
> But you must attack it directly, without hesita-
> tion or retreat, for how else can liberation
> come?

In its shorter version, this *kōan* is, "Why can't even the most enlightened person sever the red thread of passion?"

Ikkyū was one of the few Zen masters who took up Sung-yüan's challenge directly.

> Follow the rule of celibacy blindly and you are
>   no more than an ass.
> Break it and you are only human.
> The spirit of Zen is manifest in ways
>   as countless as the sands of the Ganges.
> Every newborn is a fruit of the conjugal bond.
> For how many eons have the secret blossoms
>   been budding and fading?
>
> With a young beauty, I am engrossed in fervent
>   love-play;
> We sit in the pavilion, a pleasure girl and this
>   Zen monk.
> I am enraptured by hugs and kisses
> And certainly do not feel as if I am burning in
>   hell.

In addition to the "Red thread of passion," there was another sexual *kōan* that most Zen teachers tended to avoid:

> An old woman built a hermitage for a monk and
> supported him for twenty years. One day, to test
> the extent of the monk's enlightenment, she sent
> a young girl to the hut with orders to seduce
> him. When the girl embraced the monk and
> asked, "How is this?" he replied stiffly, "A with-
> ered tree among frozen rocks; not a trace of
> warmth for three winters." Hearing of the monk's
> response, the old woman chased him out and put
> the hermitage to the torch. Why?

Ikkyū's reaction to the above *kōan* was, "If a beautiful girl were to embrace this monk, my withered willow branch would spring straight up!"

For Ikkyū, the passions were the anvil on which true enlightenment is forged.

> A sex-loving monk, you object!
> Hot-blooded and passionate, totally aroused.
> But then lust can exhaust all passion,
> Turning base metal into pure gold.

> The lotus flower
> Is not stained by the mud;
> This dewdrop form,
> Alone, just as it is,
> Manifests the real body of truth.

One day Ikkyū was traveling in an isolated area when he happened upon a naked woman preparing to bathe in a river. Ikkyū stopped, bowed reverently toward her, and continued on his way. Several passersby who witnessed this unusual scene ran after Ikkyū for an explanation of his strange behavior.

"An ordinary man would have ogled that naked woman. Why did you bow to her sex organs?" they asked.

Ikkyū replied, "Women are the source from which every being has come, including the Buddha and Bodhidharma!"

In addition to Sung-yüan, Ikkyū identified closely with two other Chinese masters, Lin-chi (Rinzai, d. 867) and, more particularly, Hsü-t'ang (Kidō, 1185–1269). Lin-chi's Zen was unadorned: "Shit and piss and just be human; when hungry, eat; when tired, sleep; make yourself the master of every situation!" Although Lin-chi did not specifically mention sex, he admonished his disciples not to "love the sacred and disdain the profane"; if they did so, they would never escape from the "whirl of samsara." Ikkyū took Lin-chi's advice: "If you are thirsty," he said, "you dream of water; if you are cold, you dream of a warm coat; as for me, I dream of the pleasures of the boudoir—that's my nature."

When Lin-chi's teacher presented him with objects symbolizing the Dharma transmission, Lin-chi unceremoniously burned them, for he detested ritual and sanctimonious behavior. Ikkyū was similarly disposed and once composed a poem entitled "I Hate Incense." He had absolutely no use for empty learning.

> A scholar-monk said to Lin-chi, "The contents of the Canon reveal Buddha-nature, don't you agree?"
> Lin-chi countered, "You haven't weeded your garden yet."

On the same theme, Ikkyū wrote:

> Every day, priests minutely examine the Law
> And endlessly chant profound sutras.
> Before this, though, they should first
> Read the love letters sent by the wind and rain,
>   the snow and moon.

Lin-chi was gruff and aggressive with irresolute students, pounding them with his fists and deafening them with ear-shattering shouts. He was truly a terror, as Ikkyū described in his inscription brushed on a portrait of the fearsome master.

> KATSU, KATSU, KATSU, KATSU!
> According to circumstance, he kills or enlivens!
> An evil devil with piercing eyes
> That see as clearly as the sun and moon.

Ikkyū considered himself one of Lin-chi's true heirs and called his favorite hermitage Katsuro-an, "Blind Donkey Hut," after Lin-chi's prophecy that his teaching would be transmitted by "blind donkeys"—stubborn, uncompromising followers of Zen who were not dazzled by fame and wealth. In that tradition Ikkyū felt free to chastise and denounce all dilettantes of Zen.

Ikkyū felt even closer to Hsü-t'ang, the Chinese teacher of Daiō, who in turn taught Daitō, the founder of the Daitoku-ji line. A wanderer and a poet, Hsü-t'ang insisted on the purity of Zen: "The Law of the Buddha consists of doing what is right and proper, not of making lavish buildings and fancy titles." Fiercely independent and not beholden to either religious or secular authorities, Hsü-t'ang was once imprisoned for resisting a government decree he considered unjust. Hsü-t'ang's death verse was simply:

> Eighty-five years
> Ignorant of Buddhism,
> Just moving steadily
> And leaving no trace in the Void.

The Records of Hsü-t'ang (Kidō roku) was Ikkyū's favorite reading. Below are Hsü-t'ang's "Three Pivot Phrases," with Ikkyū's commentary:

(1) "Lacking clear vision, how does one make cloth trousers out of thin air?"

> Paintings of rice cakes, a cruel joke, never satisfy hunger.
> Born with eyes, yet looking blind.
> In the freezing hall, conjure up the thought of clothes,
> And a cloak of the immortals will appear in the darkness.

(2) "Enclosed by a line drawn in the earth, how does one penetrate but not pass it?"

> I never tire of spring's great pleasures
> But everyone else is afraid to drain its cup.
> Heaven is achieved, hell disappears.
> I spend the day amid falling blossoms and wind blown fluff.

(3) "At the seashore you can count the sand, but
how can you stand on the point of a needle?"

Tear up the earth, count the sand, it's a big deal;
With supernatural powers you can stand on a
    needle.
Me, I'm nothing but a rustic, talentless monk,
But still I'm Hsü-t'ang's descendant in Japan.

Soon Ikkyū began signing his works, "Ikkyū, seventh-gen-
eration incarnation of Hsü-t'ang in Japan." He took to wearing
his hair long and sporting a scruffy beard like Hsü-t'ang, and
there exists an "Ikkyū as Hsü-t'ang" portrait in which the two
faces are integrated into one. Ikkyū composed this poem in
honor of Hsü-t'ang:

Abbot Hsü-t'ang snubbed the world
And cast off his robe like a useless sandal,
Unconcerned with Lin-chi's "correct transmission."
In admiration, heaven shines and bursts into
    song.

After Ikkyū fled Nyoi-an in disgust in 1440, he promulgat-
ed his dynamic, eccentric Lin-chi–Hsü-t'ang–Ikkyū style of
Zen in Kyoto and the surrounding countryside. One New
Year's Day (which was also his birthday), Ikkyū stuck a skull
on a bamboo pole and paraded through the city shouting,
"Beware, Beware!" When the festive townsfolk remonstrated
with him for trying to spoil the holiday, Ikkyū rejoined,
"Reminders of death should not mar the celebration," adding,
"I am celebrating, too," and he recited this poem:

Of all things
There is nothing
More felicitous
Than this weather-beaten
Old skull!

Ikkyū's Motto: "Entering the realm of the Buddha is easy, entering the realm of the devil is difficult." (Okayama Art Museum, Japan)
The meaning of the motto is that anyone can be a saint in the company of Buddhas, but the real challenge is to achieve awakening in the midst of the world's turmoil, suffering, and passion.

"If you understand and accept this, then you can truly celebrate New Year!" Ikkyū admonished.

When he was staying in Sakai one year, Ikkyū carried a wooden sword with him wherever he went.

"Why do you do that?" people asked. "Swords are for killing people and are hardly appropriate for a monk to carry."

Ikkyū replied, "As long as this sword is in the scabbard, it looks like the real thing and people are impressed, but if it is drawn and revealed as only a wooden stick, it becomes a joke—this is how Buddhism is these days, splendid on the surface, transparent inside."

Once a rich merchant invited a number of abbots and famous priests to a feast of vegetarian dishes. When Ikkyū showed up in his shabby robe and tattered straw hat, he was taken for a common beggar, sent around to the back, given a copper coin, and ordered to leave. The next time the merchant hosted a feast, Ikkyū attended in fancy vestments. Ikkyū removed the vestments and set them before the tray.

"What are you doing?" his host wanted to know.

"The food belongs to the robes, not to me," Ikkyū said as he was going out the door.

Every year the temples on Mount Hiei would air their huge collection of sutras, and many pilgrims visited the mountain that day to acquire merit. One year, Ikkyū was present but he fell asleep under a tree near the head temple, and a priest came over to berate him:

"Today we are airing the sacred texts! This is no place to take a nap, you sacrilegious scoundrel!"

Ikkyū stirred and then retorted, "Which is better? Buddhism printed on paper, or Buddhism in the flesh? Right now I'm airing 'Buddhism in the flesh,' so please leave me alone!"

As well as wine and women, Ikkyū loved seafood, especially octopus, and composed this verse in honor of his favorite dish:

> Lots of arms, just like Kannon the Goddess;
> Sacrificed for me, garnished with citron,
>   revere it so!

The taste of the sea, just heavenly!
Sorry, Buddha, this is one precept I can't keep.

A Kyoto pharmacist had an excellent remedy for throat ailments, but he kept the formula a closely guarded secret and charged a fortune for the medicine. Ikkyū thought this miserly and went to visit the man.

"Thousands of people could benefit from your medicine," Ikkyū told him. "It is not good to think only of yourself."

The pharmacist still refused to divulge the formula, but when Ikkyū persisted, he finally gave it to the Zen master on the condition that Ikkyū use the formula only for himself and not tell anyone the contents. Ikkyū agreed to this. As soon as he returned home, though, he put up a signboard reading:

Attention to those suffering from throat ailments!
Prepare the formula written below and you will
immediately feel better.

When the pharmacist heard of this, he was enraged and confronted Ikkyū: "You promised not to tell anyone!" he shouted.

"But I didn't speak to anyone," Ikkyū protested. "All I did was write a sign. And I've done you a big favor—if you continued to keep that formula secret, you would have ended up in hell. I've saved you from that fate."

The times were chaotic, but Ikkyū refused to sit passively in retreat. He was involved with society at all levels and practiced a fierce type of engaged Zen. The farmers were being bled dry by excessive taxation and corrupt officials, and Ikkyū would often intercede on their behalf, issuing poetic protests to the local lords.

Over and over,
Taking and taking
From this village;
Starve them
And how will *you* live?

On occasion Ikkyū also played Robin Hood. When one rich merchant died, his family planned to hold an elaborate and expensive funeral for him, but Ikkyū pilfered the money set aside for the funeral and distributed it among the poor. When the family protested, Ikkyū reprimanded them, saying, "A few pennies is enough to pay the ferryman on the River Styx. That money should be spent on the living, not the dead!"

Ikkyū addressed this poem to the authorities:

"*Cancel All Debts*"
Robbers never plunder the homes of the poor;
Private wealth does not benefit the rest of the
    nation.
Calamity has its source in the accumulated riches
    of a few,
People who lose their souls for ten thousand
    coins.

Ikkyū himself was well acquainted with the poverty that was prevalent.

"*Poem Exchanged for Food*"
Once again, I roam Higashiyama hungry.
When you are starving, a bowl of rice is worth
    a thousand pieces of gold.
One ancient worthy swapped his wisdom
    for a few lichee nuts,
Yet I can't refrain from singing odes to the wind
    and moon.

"*In Gratitude for a Gift of Soy Sauce*"
Unrestrained and free, living for thirty years,
Crazy Cloud practices his own brand of Zen.
A hundred flavors spice my simple fare:
Thin gruel and twig tea are part of the True
    Transmission.

Rather than gold and silver, Ikkyū urged his followers to acquire a *"Gentleman's Wealth"*:

> A poet's treasure consists of words and phrases;
> A scholar's days and months are perfumed with
>   books.
> Plum blossoms outside the window:
>   an unsurpassable pleasure.
> A stomach tight with cold but still enchanted by
>   snow and the moon, the frost at sunrise.

Ikkyū's concern for sentient beings extended to animals as well, and he sometimes performed funeral services for people's pets. When his own pet sparrow died, Ikkyū brushed this scroll in commemoration:

> *"Honored One of the Forest"*
> I raised a small sparrow that I loved deeply. One day it suddenly died and, grief-stricken by the loss, I decided to conduct a funeral service for my little companion just as if it were a human being. At first, I called it "Disciple Sparrow," but then upon its death I changed it to "Buddha Sparrow." Finally, I presented it with the posthumous Buddhist title "Honored One of the Forest." I composed this poem as a memorial:
>
> > A sixteen-foot Buddha body of purple and gold
> > Lies between the twin trees of Nirvana.
> > Now liberated from falsehood, beyond life
> >   and death,
> > Yet present in a thousand mountains, ten
> >   thousand trees, and hundreds of springs.

The down-to-earth, no-nonsense Zen master had many run-ins with the *yamabushi* (ascetics who practiced austerities in the mountains to attain supernatural powers). Once a big, swarthy *yamabushi* accosted Ikkyū and demanded, "What is Buddhism?"

Ikkyū replied, "The truth within one's heart."

The *yamabushi* took out a razor-sharp dagger and pointed it at Ikkyū's chest. "Well then, let's cut out yours and have a look."

Without flinching, Ikkyū countered with a poem:

> Slice open the
> Cherry trees of Yoshino
> And where will you find
> The blossoms
> That appear spring after spring?

Another time, a *yamabushi* met Ikkyū on a mountain path.

"Where are you going, Honorable Zen monk?" he inquired.

"Wherever the wind takes me," Ikkyū told the *yamabushi*.

"What happens when there is no breeze?"

"Then I make my own," Ikkyū said with a laugh as he blew on his bamboo flute.

Ikkyū was once on a ferry when a *yamabushi* challenged him.

"In the Zen sect you don't have miracles as we in the esoteric schools do."

"On the contrary," Ikkyū replied, "in Zen everyday acts are miracles."

"Is that so?" the *yamabushi* sneered. "Can you top this?"

After performing an elaborate ritual, the *yamabushi* conjured up a fiery image of Fudō Myō-ō, a fierce protector deity, in the bow of the boat. Ikkyū promptly urinated on the vision and extinguished it.

"That's a miracle issuing out of my own body," he said.

By that time the ferry had reached the shore, where a dog was running up and down and barking furiously at the passengers. The *yamabushi*, fingering his rosary and reciting incantations, tried to cast a spell on the dog, but the dog continued barking. Ikkyū pulled a tasty rice cake out of his sleeve pocket,

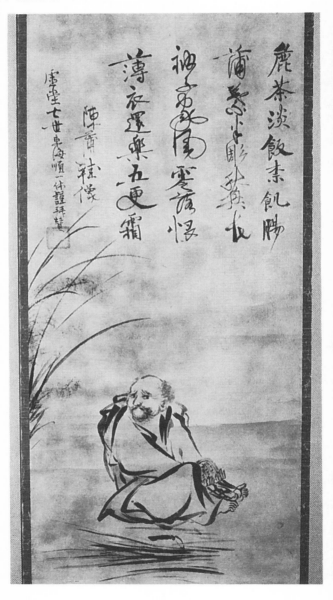

gave it to the animal, and then patted its head as the other passengers disembarked safely.

Although Ikkyū never wanted students and actually discouraged those who sought him out, he was nevertheless constantly surrounded by disciples who thrived on the austerity
and pure practice they learned under him. As he himself said,
"Hard training is the essence of the Buddhas and the Patriarchs;
Buddhas are made, not born."

Some misunderstood him, however. Ikkyū had one disciple
who copied Ikkyū's wild ways, sleeping on the altar among the
Buddha images and using pages from the sutras as toilet paper.
Ikkyū summoned him and asked, "Do you think that you are a
Buddha?"

"Yes," the disciple replied. "We are all Buddhas—you said
so yourself."

"If you are a Buddha, then why use something filthy such
as a sutra page for toilet paper? Doesn't a Buddha deserve
something better like clean, white paper?" Ikkyū then asked.
"Let me have one of your enlightened verses."

The disciple responded:

> Sitting in *zazen*
> At the Fourth
> And Fifth Avenue Bridges;

---

*Painting of the eccentric Chinese monk Chin (Ch'en), with an inscrip-
tion by Ikkyū. (Private collection, Japan)*
Iconoclastic Chin refused to have anything to do with the religious
or secular establishments of his day, eking out the barest of exis-
tences by making straw sandals, hence his nickname of "Straw Sandal" Chin. Though the painting is unsigned, it may also be by Ikkyū.
Ikkyū's inscription praises Chin as a master after his own heart:

> Twig tea and watery gruel barely keep him from
> starving,
> As he sits among the rush leaves in late autumn.
> He grieves over the spiritual failings of younger
> monks,
> His pleasure being to greet the dawn frost clad
> in a threadbare robe.

> All the people passing by,
> To me, just trees in a deep forest.

"No good!" Ikkyū shouted, and he gave this revised version:

> Sitting in *zazen*
> At the Fourth
> And Fifth Avenue Bridges;
> All the people passing by,
> To me, just as they are!

After this, the disciple stopped imitating his master's ways.

In 1444, there was a serious threat to the independence of Daitoku-ji , and Ikkyū actually joined forces with Yōsō, whom he detested, in an attempt to block the appointment of Nippō (1368–1448) as abbot of Daitoku-ji. Nippō belonged to the rival faction of Myōshin-ji, which was supported by the shoguns, while Daitoku-ji was patronized by the emperor. Ikkyū and Yōsō even rehearsed a scenario for physically (Ikkyū would block the gate) and psychologically (their penetrating questions would stop him in his tracks) preventing Nippō from assuming the abbotship. Their efforts proved fruitless, since Nippō had the backing of the powerful Hosokawa clan, henchmen of the shogun, and the Myōshin-ji usurper was finally installed as abbot. The Daitoku-ji monks continued to agitate against Nippō, however, and in 1447, when one of them committed suicide, a number of monks were made scapegoats and imprisoned. All this was too much for Ikkyū, who retired to Mount Yuzuriha, vowing to fast unto death in protest:

> I'm ashamed to remain among the living—
> I've practiced Zen and learned the Way so long
> but still all this filth.
> The Buddha's True Law has been swept away
> and destroyed,
> Replaced by Demon Kings one hundred feet tall.

Emperor Go-Hanazono (r. 1429–64) dispatched a messenger to Ikkyū bearing this plea:

> If the revered monk continues to fast, both the
> Buddha Way and the Imperial Way will perish.
> How can you forsake us? How can you desert
> the nation?

Perhaps because he had won his point by attracting the emperor's attention (and the situation did subsequently improve somewhat at Daitoku-ji), Ikkyū was persuaded to abandon his fast.

Around 1450, the temporary truce between Ikkyū and Yōsō collapsed, and the old enmity returned. Several of the aged Yōsō's disciples repudiated their master and joined Ikkyū's community, which added fuel to the fire. In 1453, a disastrous blaze destroyed much of Daitoku-ji , and when one of Yōsō's disciples was appointed abbot to oversee the reconstruction, Ikkyū's wrath was aroused. The next year, Ikkyū and Yōsō had a face-to-face confrontation, with Yōsō accusing Ikkyū of flinging "shit-water" in their master Kasō's face by his wild behavior and his constant criticism of Kasō's legitimate heirs. Ikkyū countered that Yōsō's followers never mentioned the hunger and hardship that Daitō and the other Daitoku-ji patriarchs suffered in their search for true Zen but dwelled instead on the influence they had over aristocrats and shoguns, and the grand edifices erected in their names.

> [Ikkyū] speaks of Daitō's unsurpassed brilliance
> But the clatter of royal carriages drowns him out,
> And no one listens to tales of the Patriarch's
> Long years of hunger and homelessness at Fifth
>   Avenue Bridge.

After this abusive encounter, neither man spoke to the other again, although Ikkyū kept up his attacks in vitriolic poems and other public pronouncements. Ikkyū, of all people, even condemned Yōsō for running around with women, and he rejoiced when Yōsō died in 1458 of what Ikkyū said could only have been leprosy, the just reward for heretics and evildoers. Thoroughly disgusted at all the squabbling with Yōsō and his heirs, from 1461 Ikkyū temporarily abandoned Zen and joined the Pure Land Sect for a few months.

> Crazy Cloud is a demon in Daitō's line,
> But he hates this hellish bickering.
> What good are old *kōan* and dated precedents?
> No use complaining. I'll just rely on my inner
>   treasures.

What were the reasons for Ikkyū's intractable hatred of Yōsō? The two were the keenest of rivals when they were fellow students of Kasō, and Ikkyū certainly felt, with much justification, that he was far more talented than Yōsō, who was his senior. Yet it was Yōsō who was publicly acknowledged as Kasō's chief disciple and was twice appointed abbot of Daitoku-ji. The singular title "The Wise One, Great Light Zen Master" was also bestowed on him by the emperor. (Ikkyū switched the ideograms in that title to read, "The Filthy One, Burning with Lust Zen Master.") Another source of friction was their characters, which were diametrically opposed: Ikkyū was mercurial, uncompromising, and radical; Yōsō was conciliatory, cautious, and conservative. To Ikkyū, Yōsō, despite all his worldly honors, was nothing more than an ecclesiastical puppet devoid of true inspiration and understanding, and he personified everything that Ikkyū abhorred in the world of Zen. Nevertheless, Ikkyū's animosity appears excessive and reveals a defect in his personality.

Since Ikkyū lived during one of the most turbulent periods in Japanese history—a constant cycle of famine, plague, rice riots, and wars—perhaps his intolerance is understandable. In addition to the death and destruction going on around him, Ikkyū had continual skirmishes with his fellow clerics, accusing them of perverting Buddhism for the sake of wealth and fame. Given such a gloomy environment, in 1457 the sixty-three-year-old pessimist felt compelled to compose *Skeletons* (*Gaikotsu*), which became his best-known work and is still read and studied today:

These thin lines of Indian ink reveal all truth.

Students, sit earnestly in *zazen*, and you will realize that everything born in this world is ultimately empty, including oneself and the original face of existence. All things indeed emerge out of emptiness. This original formlessness is the "Buddha," and all other similar terms—Buddha-nature, Buddhahood, Buddha-mind, Awakened One, Patriarch, God—are merely different expressions for the same emptiness. Misunderstand this and you will end up in hell.

Filled with disgust and longing to liberate myself from the realm of continual birth and death, I left home and set off on a journey. One night, as I was looking for a place to rest, I came upon a lonely little temple. It was at the base of a mountain far from the main road, seemingly lost in a vast Plain of Repose. The temple was in a field of graves, and suddenly a pitiful-looking skeleton appeared and said these words:

A melancholy autumn wind
Blows through the world;
The pampas grass waves,
As we drift to the moor,
Drift to the sea.

What can be done
With the mind of a man
That should be clear
But though he is dressed up in a monk's robe,
Just lets life pass him by?

All things become naught by returning to their origin. Bodhidharma faced the wall in meditation, but none of the thoughts that arose in his mind had any reality. The same holds true for the Buddha's fifty years of proclaiming the Law. The mind is not bound by such conditioned things.

Such deep musings made me uneasy, and I could not sleep. Toward dawn I dozed off, and in my dream I found myself surrounded by a group of skeletons, acting as they had when they were still alive. One skeleton came over to me and said:

> Memories
> Flee and
> Are no more.
> All are empty dreams
> Devoid of meaning.

> Violate the reality of things
> And babble about
> "God" and "the Buddha"
> And you will never find
> The true Way.

> Still breathing,
> You feel animated,
> So a corpse in a field
> Seems to be something
> Apart from you.

I liked this skeleton—he had renounced the world to seek the truth and had passed from the shallows to the depths. He saw things clearly, just as they are. I lay there with the wind in the pines whispering in my ears and the autumn moonlight dancing across my face.

What is not a dream? Who will not end up as a

skeleton? We appear as skeletons covered with skin—male and female—and lust after each other. When the breath expires, though, the skin ruptures, sex disappears, and there is no more high or low. Underneath the skin of the person we fondle and caress right now is nothing more than a set of bare bones. Think about it—high and low, young and old, male and female, all are the same. Awaken to this one great matter and you will immediately comprehend the meaning of "unborn and undying."

If chunks of rock
Can serve as a memento
To the dead,
A better headstone
Would be a simple tea-mortar.

Humans are indeed frightful beings.

A single moon
Bright and clear
In an unclouded sky;
Yet still we stumble
In the world's darkness.

Have a good look—stop the breath, peel off the skin, and everybody ends up looking the same. No matter how long you live the result is not altered [even for emperors]. Cast off the notion that "I exist." Entrust yourself to the wind-blown clouds, and do not wish to live for ever.

This world
Is but
A fleeting dream
So why be alarmed
At its evanescence?

Your span of life is set and all entreaties to the gods to lengthen it are to no avail. Keep your mind fixed on the one great matter [of life and death]. Life ends in death, that's the way things are.

The vagaries of life,
Though painful,
Teach us
Not to cling
To this floating world.

Why do people
Lavish decoration
On this set of bones,
Destined to disappear
Without a trace?

The original body
Must return to
Its original place.
Do not search
For what cannot be found.

No one really knows
The nature of birth
Nor the true dwelling place.
We return to the source
And turn to dust.

Many paths lead from
The foot of the mountain,
But at the peak
We all gaze at the
Single bright moon.

If at the end of our journey
There is no final

Resting place,
Then we need not fear
Losing our Way.

No beginning,
No end.
Our mind
Is born and dies:
The emptiness of emptiness!

Relax,
And the mind
Runs wild;
Control the world
And you can cast it aside.

Rain, hail, snow, and ice:
All are different,
But when they fall
They become the same water
As the valley stream.

The ways of proclaiming
The Mind all vary,
But the same heavenly truth
Can be seen
In each and every one.

Cover your path
With fallen pine needles
So no one will be able
To locate your
True dwelling place.

How vain,
The endless funerals at the
Cremation grounds of Mount Toribe!

Don't the mourners realize
That they will be next?

"Life is fleeting!"
We think at the sight
Of smoke drifting from Mount Toribe,
But when will we realize
That we are in the same boat?

All is in vain!
This morning,
A healthy friend;
This evening,
A wisp of cremation smoke.

What a pity!
Evening smoke from Mount Toribe
Blown violently
To and fro
By the wind.

When burned,
We become ashes,
And earth when buried.
Is it only our sins
That remain behind?

All the sins
Committed
In the Three Worlds
Will fade away
Together with me.

This is how the world is. Those who have not
grasped the world's impermanence are astonished
and terrified by such a change. Few today seek Buddhist truth, and the monasteries are largely empty.

Priests now are mostly ignorant and shun *zazen* as bothersome; they are derelict in their meditation, concentrating instead on decorating their temples. Their *zazen* is a sham, and they are merely masquerading as monks—the robes they sport will become heavy coats of torture someday.

Within the cosmos of birth and death, the taking of life leads to hell; greed leads to rebirth as a hungry ghost; ignorance causes one to be reborn as an animal; anger turns one into a demon. Follow the precepts and you attain rebirth as a human being. Do good deeds and you ascend to the level of the gods. Above these six realms there are the four levels of the Wise Buddhas, altogether ten realms of existence. However, one enlightened thought reveals them all to be formless, with nothing in between, and not to be loathed, feared, or desired. Existence is perceived as being nothing more than a wispy cloud in the vast sky, or foam on water. No thoughts arise in the mind, so no elements are created. Mind and object are one, yet perfectly empty.

Human birth is like a fire—the father is the flint, the mother is the stone, and the resultant spark is the child. The fire is ignited with the base elements and burns until it exhausts the fuel. The lovemaking between the father and mother produces the spark of life. Since the parents are without beginning, they too flicker out; all things emerge from emptiness— the source of every form. Free yourself from forms and return to the original ground of being. From this ground, life issues forth, but let go of this, too.

> Break open
> A cherry tree
> And there are no flowers,
> But the spring breeze
> Brings forth a myriad blossoms!

Without a bridge
Clouds climb effortlessly
To heaven;
No need to rely on
Anything Gotama Buddha taught.

Gotama Buddha proclaimed the Law for fifty years, and when his disciple Kāśyapa asked him for the key to his teaching, the Buddha said, "From beginning to end I have not proclaimed a single word," and held up a flower. Kāśyapa smiled, and the Buddha gave him the flower, saying these words: "You possess the wondrous mind of the True Law." "What do you mean?" asked Kāśyapa. "My fifty years of preaching," the Buddha told him, "has been beckoning to you all the while, just like attracting a child into one's arms with the promise of a reward."

This flower of the Buddhist Law cannot be described in physical, mental, or verbal terms. It is not material or spiritual. It is not intellectual knowledge. Our Law is the Flower of the One Vehicle, carrying all the Buddhas of the Past, Present, and Future. It holds the twenty-eight Indian and six Chinese Patriarchs; it is the original ground of being—all there is. All things are without beginning and are thus all-inclusive. The eight senses, the four seasons, the four great elements (earth, water, fire, wind), all originate in emptiness, but few realize it. Wind is breath, fire is animation, water is blood; when the body is buried or burned it becomes earth. Yet these elements, too, are without beginning, and do not abide.

In this world,
All things, without exception,
Are unreal.

Death itself is
An illusion.

Delusion makes it appear that though the body
dies, the soul endures—this is a grave error. The
enlightened declare that both body and soul perish
together. "Buddha" is emptiness, and heaven and
earth return to the original ground of being. I've set
aside the 80,000 books of scripture and given you
the essence in this slim volume. This will bring you
great bliss.

Writing something
To leave behind
Is yet another kind of dream.
When I awake I know that
There will be no one to read it.

Ikkyū's Buddhism was not always as dark and gloomy as
this; even in the worst of times, there were periods suffused
with light and graced by sublime beauty. He once wrote, "Joy
in the midst of suffering is the mark of Ikkyū's school."

The appreciation—the savoring—of beauty in all its forms
was at the heart of Ikkyū's message, and he is in many ways
the godfather of the Zen arts.

With the exception of *Skeletons*, Ikkyū's prose works are
didactic and surprisingly conventional, but his fiery Zen poetry
is the finest of the genre. Ikkyū was well aware that the old-
time Zen masters denounced literature and poetry as the
devices of hell:

Monks these days study hard in order to turn
A fine phrase and win fame as talented poets.
At Crazy Cloud's hut there is no talent,
    but there is lots of flavor,
As he boils a cup of rice in a battered old cauldron.

Still, Ikkyū's obsession with poetry would not abate:

> Bliss and sorrow; love and hate; light and shadow;
>   heat and cold; happiness and anger; self and other.
> The enjoyment of poetic beauty may well lead to
>   hell.
> But look what we find strewn along our path:
> Plum blossoms and peach flowers!

Sterile versification, clever wordplay, and literary pretentiousness stifle Zen, but Ikkyū's "crazy" poems were manifestations of Zen. He revealed himself completely in his wild, untrammeled verse, recording his ecstasy and despair, his loves and hates, his humanity and Buddhahood, with the unflinching honesty and directness demanded of true Zen.

Most of Ikkyū's poems were written in the Chinese style of verse (*kanshi*), but he also composed Japanese verses (*waka*) and greatly influenced Sōgi (1421–1502), a central figure in the history of Japanese poetry who studied Zen with him and imbibed the Ikkyū style: refined yet bold, direct, and penetrating. Ikkyū can also be considered the patron saint of haiku, satirical *senryū*, and madcap *kyōka*, which developed later. Linked verse—impromptu compositions in which one poet would start the verse with a 5/7/5-syllable form to be capped with a 7/7 syllable verse by another poet—eventually evolved into haiku, which was the initial 5/7/5 verse treated independently as the shortest and sweetest expression of Buddhist

---

Daruma (Bodhidharma), by Ikkyū's disciple Bokkei, with an inscription by Ikkyū. (Okayama Art Museum, Japan)
Spare, austere, and intense, the brushwork displayed here well conveys Ikkyū-style Zen. The inscription refers to the tale of Eka (Hui-k'e) standing outside Daruma's cave for days in the snow to prove his sincerity.

> Who else can set his mind at rest?
> Long ago Shinkō [Eka] stood at Shōrin-ji
> Unaware of the snow piling up around him,
> While Daruma faced the wall, not revealing his face.

truth, a decisive kind of the "Zen shout" Ikkyū always advocated. Ikkyū's example, in life and in his verse, provided ample precedent and inspiration for the biting satire of *senryū* and the zaniness of *kyōka*, "mad verse."

In the Far East, calligraphy is deemed the ultimate art form, and Ikkyū's brushwork is unrivaled for its intensity and wild abandon. It bristles with fierce energy and flows like a series of rapids, vibrant and compelling. Ikkyū's calligraphy demands the viewer's full attention, and one can receive a real sense of the depth of Crazy Cloud's Zen when confronting his brushwork.

Ikkyū also painted, and he had a guiding hand in the development of the Soga school. His stern and simple ink paintings also give the viewer no quarter, even though they are usually on a smaller scale than his calligraphic works. Ikkyū was the first master to fully utilize calligraphy and painting as a vehicle for transmitting Zen teachings. Following Ikkyū's example, calligraphy and painting—visual sermons—became a primary form of the "skillful means" employed by all the great masters to inspire and instruct Zen students.

Here are a few examples of how calligraphy can become a Zen tool. A simple but sincere farmer once came to Ikkyū with this question: "Some priests tell us that at death we will go to the Paradise of the Pure Land. Others say we will be reborn, becoming a human or a beast depending on the good and evil we did in life. What's the truth?" Ikkyū brushed this poem in easy-to-read *kana* script for the farmer to hang in his alcove:

> If there is no one
> Before your
> Birth,
> Then there is nowhere
> To go at death.

The farmer had the calligraphy mounted, and every morning he would meditate before the scroll. One day, he understood the message: Live in the here and now, and don't worry about the rest!

Another time, sales were low at a shop selling fans run by an elderly couple and they were in danger of losing everything, so they came to Ikkyū for help. He told them, "Adopt me as your son for a few days." They did so, and Ikkyū placed this sign in front of their shop: "Ikkyū has been adopted into this family, and in celebration tomorrow he will autograph any fan purchased here." The news spread like wildfire, and the following day the shop was swamped with customers. The couple sold a year's worth of fans in a single day, and the business was saved.

The chief abbot of Mount Hiei also requested some calligraphy from Ikkyū for the temple, but Ikkyū found the abbot a bit pompous, so he gave him a scrap of paper with a mess of illegible scribbles on it. When the abbot politely asked for something a bit grander and more legible, Ikkyū told him to gather all the paper he could and get hold of the biggest brush possible. Ikkyū then had the paper glued together in one enormous long sheet that extended from one side of the mountain to the other. He filled the brush with ink, sped down one side of the paper drawing a long line, refilled the brush, and then came back up the other side.

"What does it say?" the abbot asked sheepishly.

"Why s*hi*, of course," Ikkyū said with a chuckle. (This symbol is perhaps the simplest in the Japanese *kana* syllabary.)

Ikkyū's influence on *sadō*, the Way of Tea, was profound and lasting. Ikkyū believed that the preparation and drinking of tea should function as Zen in action; and that the tea ceremony was more than a pleasant pastime or an opportunity for the ostentatious display of expensive antiques imported from mainland China. Tea drinking must be grounded in Zen aesthetics: *fūryū* (deep awareness of the essential), *wabi* (austere beauty, appreciation of the natural and unadorned), *sabi* (appreciation of the aged and mellow, solitary and tranquil), and *shibui* (a taste for the astringent and understated). Ikkyū further stated that the tea ceremony should harmonize the best of Chinese and Japanese taste.

By being the first to commission ceramics suitable for the

tea ceremony from local kilns, Ikkyū also spurred the development of Japanese pottery. Ikkyū was the teacher of Murata Shukō (1422–1502), Japan's first official tea master, and the scroll Ikkyū presented Shukō of calligraphy by the Chinese master Yüan-wu (Engo, 1063–1135) was the one displayed at Shukō's initial tea gatherings. This inaugurated the custom of hanging a work by a Zen master in the alcove during the ceremony. (That particular scroll is still treasured as the granddaddy of all Zen tea art.) Shukō and the monk Jōtei (thought to have been Ikkyū's son) transmitted these ideals to Takeno Jōō (1502–55), who in turn passed them on to Sen no Rikyū (1522–91), patriarch of the modern schools of tea in Japan.

The illustrious Noh actor Konparu Zenchiku (1405–68) studied Zen with Ikkyū to improve his mind and his dramatic performance. Ever since, Zen has been associated with Noh: a master actor must capture perfect stillness in the midst of movement and harmonize his body and mind with the chorus and audience so well that they become one. Two Noh dramas, *Eguchi* and *Yamauba*, have also been attributed—without conclusive proof—to Ikkyū.

Ikkyū also knew the exquisite beauty of love. The May to December romance between the young blind minstrel Lady

Ikkyū and His Lover Lady Mori. (Masaki Art Museum, Japan)
Above his own portrait, Ikkyū wrote:

> Within this Zen circle, my entire body is revealed.
> This is really a painting of Kidō's incarnation.
> My blind minstrel sings of love and makes
>   this old rascal smile—
> One tune with her beneath the flowers is like
>   ten thousand springs.

Next to Lady Mori's image Ikkyū brushed her poignant poem describing their May–December romance:

> In the gap between
> Deep dreams and light sleep
> I float and sink—
> There is no way to staunch
> My flow of bittersweet tears.

Mori and the old abbot is one of the most celebrated in Japanese history. When he first met her, Ikkyū wrote:

> The most beautiful and truest of all women;
> Her songs the fresh, pure melody of love.
> A voice and a sweet smile that rend my heart:
> I'm in a spring forest of lovely crab apples.

Hopelessly smitten, the two became inseparable.

> Every night, Blind Mori accompanies me in song.
> Under the covers, two mandarin ducks whisper
>   to each other.
> We promise to be together for ever,
> But right now this old fellow enjoys an eternal
>   spring.

> By a river or the sea, or in the mountains,
> A man of the Way shuns fame and fortune.
> Night after night, we two lovebirds snuggle on
>   the meditation platform,
> Lost in dalliance, intimate talk, and orgasmic
>   bliss.

Ikkyū evidently fathered a love-child with Mori, and he composed this poem for his daughter:

> Even among beauties she is a precious pearl,
> A little princess in this sorry world.
> She is the inevitable result of true love,
> And a Zen master is no match for her!

While Ikkyū's association with the Zen arts bore splendid fruit during his sixties and seventies, the dark and desperate situation in Kyoto worsened. In the senseless ten-year Ōnin War (1467–77), Kyoto was destroyed and abandoned to the dead. Both Katsuro-an and Daitoku-ji went up in flames in the first year of the conflict, and Ikkyū sought refuge initially at Shūon-an, a small temple that he had founded, and then at other retreats in the area. Ikkyū was frequently ill the last two decades of his life, plagued by terrible bouts of diarrhea.

In a complete turnaround for both Ikkyū and the monastic establishment, the iconoclast "Crazy Cloud" monk was appointed abbot of Daitoku-ji in 1474, at the age of eighty. Despite his loathing of sham monks, institutional Buddhism, and Zen formalism, Ikkyū cherished the original ideals of Daitoku-ji, and he did not want its physical presence to vanish from the world. With the entire complex in ruins, the monastic establishment had nowhere else to turn. Ikkyū was well aware of the contradiction:

> *"Upon Becoming Abbot of Daitoku-ji"*
> Daitō's descendants have nearly extinguished
>   his light;
> After such a long, cold night, the chill will be
>   difficult to melt with my love songs.
> For fifty years, a vagabond in a straw raincoat
>   and hat,
> Now mortified as a purple-robed abbot.

Ikkyū was serious about rebuilding Daitoku-ji, but he was not about to change his ways. He allowed himself to get decked out in the full regalia of his office for a formal portrait, but when it was finished he added this inscription:

> Crazy fellow, stirring up a mad wind;
> Wandering about for years in brothels and wine
>   shops.
> Anyone here care to match wits with me?
> You can sketch me in the south, the north,
>   the east [– and I won't change a bit]!

Yet Ikkyū was able to accomplish the impossible. With his large circle of contacts, and with his many patrons and his monastic and lay followers laboring in unison, Daitoku-ji was completely rebuilt in seven years.

The effort exhausted the octogenarian, though, and he weakened year by year. Near the end of his life he told his disciples, "After my death some of you will seclude yourselves in the forests and mountains to meditate, while others may drink saké and enjoy the company of women. Both kinds of Zen are fine, but if some become professional clerics, babbling about 'Zen as the Way,' they are my enemies. I have never given an *inka*, and if anyone claims to have received such a thing from me, have him or her arrested!"

Ikkyū was as eccentric in death as in life, as several death verses attributed to him show:

> I won't die,
> I won't go anywhere,
> But I won't be here.
> So don't ask me anything—
> For I won't answer!

> Dimly, dimly, thirty years;
> Faintly, faintly, thirty years;
> Dimly, faintly, sixty years.
> I pass my feces and offer them to Brahma.

Then there is this touching farewell poem to Lady Mori:

> Ten years ago beneath the blossoms we began a
>   fragrant alliance.
> Each stage was a delight, full of endless passion.
> How poignant, never again to pillow my head
>   on her lap.
> Making sweet love together, we vowed to be
>   together always.

Ikkyū's actual death verse, apparently brushed just hours before he passed away on the twenty-first day of the eleventh month of 1481, as he was sitting in the lotus posture, goes:

> In this vast universe,
> Who understood my Zen?
> Even if Hsü-t'ang himself came back
> He would not be worth half a penny!

Bokusai, Ikkyū's long-time disciple and first biographer, eulogized his master as follows: "Ikkyū did not distinguish between the high and low in society, and he enjoyed mingling with artisans, merchants, and children. Youngsters followed him about, and birds came to eat out of his hands. Whatever possessions he received he passed on to others. He was strict and demanding but treated all without favoritism. Ikkyū laughed heartily when he was happy and shouted mightily when angry."

HAKUIN EKAKU
(1686–1768)

UNLIKE Ikkyū's case, much autobiographical material is found in Hakuin's own works, for he is one of the few Zen masters that has described his youth and initial search for the Way in some detail. Hakuin's family ran an inn and served as the postmasters of Hara, a village lying at the foot of Mount Fuji and a way station on the old Tōkaidō, the highway running from Edo (Tokyo) to Kyoto.

Right from his birth in 1686, his mother felt that her fifth child and third son was special. "You were born in the ox-year, in the ox-month, on the ox-day, at the ox-hour," she told him. The ox is the sacred animal of Tenjin (the deified form of Sugawara no Michizane, 845–903, patron of literature and learning), and Hakuin became a lifelong devotee of that auspicious deity. For some reason, Hakuin did not walk until he was two, but by the age of three the suddenly precocious child had memorized every word of all the nursery rhymes and folk songs he had heard. At the age of four, a visit to the seashore and the sight of the endlessly flowing waves and the drifting clouds made the serious little boy burst into tears—he intuitively understood the world's impermanence.

The boy spent much of his childhood eagerly accompanying his mother on her visits to local temples to listen to Buddhist sermons, and amazed his family by repeating verbatim

what he had heard. A holy man once visited the family, proph-
esied great things for the unusual child, and then imparted this
sage advice to Hakuin:

> (1) Don't waste food; mix a little hot water with
> anything left over [in your bowl] and eat it;
> (2) Always urinate while squatting;
> (3) The north is sacred, so don't desecrate it by
> urinating, defecating, or sitting with your back
> or stretching your legs out in that direction. And
> never forget the six years Buddha spent fasting
> in the Himalayas and the nine years Daruma sat
> in a cave. Observe these three precepts, learn to
> concentrate like Buddha and Daruma, and you
> will be blessed with a long life.

Following this encounter with the holy man, it is said that
Hakuin faithfully followed these injunctions to the end of his
days.

When he was ten years old, Hakuin and his pious mother
attended a vivid sermon given by a Nichiren priest on the tor-
ments of hell. Even years later Hakuin recalled that the dreadful words froze his liver with fear and caused him to tremble in
terror for days. He immediately stopped fighting with his play-
mates, and was stricken with remorse for having killed insects
and teased small animals to death. Not long after that fire-and-
brimstone sermon, Hakuin took a bath with his mother, who
loved the water steaming hot. The crackling wood, the shooting
sparks, and the hissing of the water on the metal conjured up
the memory of hell so forcefully that he screamed in panic.
After calming down, he confessed to his mother that he was
terrified of falling into the flames of hell. She encouraged her
apprehensive son to pray to Tenjin, his guardian angel, for
deliverance. Thereafter, it was Hakuin's practice to arise every
night at the ox-hour (2:00 A.M.) to venerate Tenjin with
incense, flowers, and prayer.

Despite his assiduous devotion, Hakuin still worried that

Tenjin might fail to protect him if he found himself in a difficult situation. Once one of the boy's toy arrows badly missed
the mark and hit a valuable painting hanging in the alcove in
his home. After being punished for this deed, Hakuin fretted
that, "If Tenjin can't help me in a small matter like this, how
can he protect me from damnation in hell?" That evening he
shut his eyes and said, "Tenjin! If you truly possess the power
to deliver me from hell, please make the incense smoke rise in
a straight line. If not, let it swirl about." He opened his eyes and
the smoke was rising in a line. Shutting his eyes and reciting a
prayer of gratitude, he opened them again to find the smoke
wafting in every direction. Totally confused, he then decided to
couple his worship of Tenjin with that of Kannon, Goddess of
Compassion, a Buddhist deity reputed to possess great powers
of salvation.

However, even backed by the combined power of Tenjin
and Kannon, Hakuin continued to fear eternal damnation. At a
temple festival Hakuin saw a puppet play on the miracles of the
Nichiren priest Nisshin (1407–88), who supposedly walked
into a blazing fire without being burned and was submerged
in water without being drowned. "That's the key," Hakuin
thought. "If I renounce the world and join the religious life, I
will surely be saved." While his mother approved, his father
believed that such a step was premature, so the boy immersed
himself in his studies instead, committing such weighty texts as
the Confucian classics, the *Diamond Sutra*, and the *Collection
of Zen Words and Phrases (Kuzōshi)* to memory over the next
three years.

Hakuin also took to secluding himself in the mountains, far
removed from the noise and confusion of regular daily life. He
carved an image of Kannon out of the trunk of a tree and spent
hours chanting sutras and doing *zazen* before it. Once a flash
flood cut him off from the village. When the water level had
not subsided after two days, the impatient Hakuin stripped off
his clothes, which he tied in a bundle and placed on his shoulder, and jumped into the raging torrent, brandishing his small
sword to ward off any monsters that might emerge. After arriv-

ing home safely, he told his anxious parents, "I couldn't wait any longer—time is precious and I can't waste a minute in my quest."

In 1699, when he was thirteen, both his parents finally gave their consent and Hakuin was ordained a Zen monk by Tanrei (d. 1701), abbot of Shōin-ji, a local temple that had been restored by Hakuin's great-uncle. Hakuin vowed to train until he attained the ability to remain unscathed by fire and immune to drowning.

Immediately after his ordination, Hakuin was sent to train under the scholar-monk Sokudō (d. 1712) at the nearby temple of Daishō-ji. There Hakuin studied the *Lotus Sutra*, which seemed to him to be no more than a collection of fairy tales and simple parables. Never one to accept any doctrine passively, Hakuin posed this question to Sokudō: "I left my parents to study Buddhism. The *Lotus Sutra* is supposed to be the 'King of Buddhist texts,' but apart from the teaching of the 'One Vehicle' [in which all types of Buddhist practice are harmonized] it mostly contains things that can be found in the Chinese classics, music books, and even geisha songs. What then is the value of Buddhism?" Sokudō had no ready answers, but he did praise his student's intense desire to discover the truth for himself.

In 1703, the seventeen-year-old boy decided to go on pilgrimage as an *unsui*, "a monk drifting with the clouds and flowing with the water, in search of the Way." He first went to a monastery called Zensō-ji, where he heard the abbot speak one day of Yen-t'ou (Gantō, 828–87), a famous Chinese Zen master. Once, Yen-t'ou and his group of monks were set upon by highwaymen. While the other monks fled in terror, Yen-t'ou calmly sat down in the *zazen* posture. When he was murdered by the bandits, his screams could be heard from miles away. "If such a virtuous priest could suffer so," Hakuin said, "what's in store for the likes of me? Surely there is nothing more worthless than a Buddhist monk!" Hakuin's predicament threw him into acute agitation, and he was unable to eat or sleep for days. Finally, he concluded in despair that he was doomed to hell and that it was pointless to worry about his fate. Since he was too embarrassed to return home in abject failure, he decided at least to make a name for himself in literature.

While Hakuin was at Zensō-ji, a local girl fell in love with him after a chance meeting in the village. Her parents offered to adopt Hakuin into the family and urged him to give up his monastic vows to marry their daughter. Hakuin was indeed attracted to the girl, but he resisted the temptation, recalling the many vows he had made never to waver in his quest. (The girl passed away a few years later, and after Hakuin founded Ryū-taku-ji, a memorial tablet for her was enshrined in the temple.)

In 1704, Hakuin heard of a monk called Baō (1629–1711), who was reputed to have no equal in the field of poetry. Baō was abbot of Zuiun-ji, a little temple in Mino in central Honshū, and Hakuin arrived there with a group of twelve monks. Within a few months, though, the poverty of the temple and Baō's harsh discipline had defeated everyone but Hakuin. As the monks were preparing to flee, Baō came over to Hakuin and said, "Well, they are flying the coop. How about you?" Hakuin reassured Baō that he would never give up.

Once alone with that demanding teacher, Hakuin made rapid progress with his poetry, but again he was assailed by self-doubt: "Even if my verse surpasses that of the master Li Po (701–62) or Tu Fu (712–70), that won't help me a whit when I have to face the King of Hell!" Hakuin went to the temple veranda where the monastic books were being aired and prayed, "Buddhas and gods! Help me in my quest and indicate the path I should follow!" He closed his eyes and picked out a book at random. It was *Smashing Through the Zen Barrier (Zenkan sakushin).* He opened the text to the story of the Chinese monk Tz'u-ming (Jimyō, 987–1040). When Tz'u-ming felt drowsiness overtake him during his all-night meditation sessions, he gouged his thigh with a gimlet to regain his concentration. When asked why he was so hard on himself, the monk said, "Through severe discipline the ancients grew illustrious. To achieve nothing in one's lifetime and die without any accomplishments is a terrible waste. That is why I pierce my thigh." Hakuin, greatly encouraged by this dramatic tale, became more determined than ever to persevere.

During his stay at Baō's temple, Hakuin's mother died, but he was unable to return for her funeral. In 1705, the nineteen-year-old monk left Zuiun-ji to join the community of Nanzen (1662–1710) for the summer training period. There Hakuin became acquainted with and immediately developed a strong distaste for "Ordinary" (or "Unborn") Zen, a type of low-key, go-with-the-flow Buddhism that eschewed reliance on any form of regulated practice or strict discipline.

The next year Hakuin discovered the *Sayings of Hsü-t'ang*, containing the teachings of the Chinese master who had so inspired Ikkyū. Hakuin traveled to Jōkō-ji to attend a series of lectures on this text given by the abbot Banri (1650–1713). Through the talks, he learned of other monks who had agonized over their lack of progress and apparent madness, yet had persevered to experience at last "the great bliss that follows on great misery."

In the summer of 1706, Hakuin went south to train at Shōshū-ji in Shikoku and was subsequently invited to visit the local lord's castle. There he was shown a collection of scrolls and was struck by one special treasure. It was the calligraphy of a Zen monk (either Daigū [1584–1669] or Ungo [1582–1659], depending on the account)—vigorous, radiant, and compelling, yet perfectly natural and not at all self-conscious. Thinking that, "This brushwork is the result of true enlightenment; it has nothing to do with technique," Hakuin returned to the temple and, totally disgusted with the pretense of his efforts, burned all his brushes and samples of calligraphy. He was not to pick up a brush seriously again until he was nearly sixty.

Instead, Hakuin dedicated himself to training with renewed vigor: "I'll be like a log floating full speed down a river, neither getting caught along the banks and rotting away nor relying on the help of men or gods, but moving ever onward until I reach the ocean!"

Hakuin then became engrossed in the first great barrier of

Zen, the *kōan* "*Mu*" (Naught!). While he struggled with this riddle, Hakuin felt as if he had entered a pitch-black cave. In 1707, when the twenty-one-year-old monk was walking in a picturesque district by the Inland Sea, his companions urged him to enjoy the magnificent views. However, Hakuin did not so much as raise his eyes: "I still have not attained the Way. How can I have time for sightseeing?" Yet when the party reached Kaisei-ji in Nishinomiya, Hakuin composed this optimistic verse:

> Beneath the mountain a stream flows
> On and on without end.
> If one's Zen mind is like this
> Seeing into one's own nature cannot be far off.

When Hakuin received word that Baō was ill, he returned to Zuiun-ji to nurse his teacher. During the day Hakuin practiced meditation in action—cleaning, gardening, cooking, and tending his sick master—and at night he practiced meditation in stillness, sitting hour after hour in *zazen*. In his meditations he was disturbed by visions: some were of awful demons, and others had him soaring among the clouds and flying across the four seas. In a few months Baō recovered and, after an absence of four and a half years, Hakuin returned to his home town of Hara. Although he was besieged with questions from his relatives and friends about his long pilgrimage, he gave only noncommittal grunts in response. Everyone agreed that he had changed.

Near the end of 1707, Mount Fuji erupted. Lava spewed into the sky, the earth shook violently, and volcanic ash rained down on the village. Hakuin was staying at Shōin-ji, and several family members went to rescue him, only to find him sitting in *zazen*. He refused to budge: "If I attain enlightenment, I'll be protected; if I don't, it's no loss if I perish—I'm entrusting myself to heaven." Hakuin survived the disaster unharmed.

In 1708, Hakuin traveled to Echigo, a province along the Sea of Japan, to attend a series of lectures on the book *Dharma*

Eye of Men and Gods (Ninten ganmoku). Disappointed at the lecturer's superficial understanding of the text and his own difficulties with meditation, Hakuin shut himself up in a shrine near the temple and commenced a seven-day retreat of fasting and *zazen.* He recorded that he felt frozen solid in a sheet of ice extending ten thousand leagues. Midway during the retreat, at midnight he heard the sound of a bell in the distance and felt his "body and mind drop away." He shouted at the top of his lungs, "Yen-t'ou [Gantō, the murdered monk] is right here, alive and well!" Fearing someone in the neighborhood was suffering the same fate as Yen-t'ou, the startled monks ran to the shrine, only to find Hakuin beaming with joy.

Despite Hakuin's low regard for the lectures, more than five hundred people attended them. One day, a wild-looking monk over six feet tall and brandishing a huge staff appeared. Everyone was terrified of him, but Hakuin agreed to act as his guide. Once the lectures began, however, the gigantic monk displayed remarkable understanding of the matters being discussed. To Hakuin, the monk represented a "fresh rain after a long drought," and the two spent hours swapping Zen stories. The monk, whose name was Kaku (1679–1730), offered to introduce Hakuin to his master Shōju, a crusty old hermit living in the mountains of Iiyama (present-day Nagano Prefecture). Hakuin and Kaku left the series of lectures and made their way to Shōju's ramshackle hut.

Shōju (1642–1721) was the disciple and sole heir of Bunan (1603–76), a demanding Zen master who had lived most of his life as a layman. Bunan had given his trainees no respite, constantly exhorting them:

> Die while alive,
> Be completely dead!
> Then do
> What you will
> And all will be well.

Shōju, too, was notoriously severe on himself—once he spent

an entire week meditating every night in a cemetery that was surrounded by a pack of hungry wolves.

Shōju is best known for his "Thrashing of the Master Swordsman." Swordsmen often sought the counsel of Zen masters in the hope of discovering a means of harmonizing technique and spirit. Once, one such swordsman approached Shōju, who listened politely to the swordsman's theories and digressions for some time before suddenly leaping up and pummeling him unmercifully. By experiencing Zen in a most direct and forceful manner, the swordsman was enlightened about the ultimate principle of his art.

News of Shōju's "no-holds-barred" Zen created a stir, and he was invited to watch a training session for master swordsmen. The assembled swordsmen professed admiration of Shōju's profound understanding of Zen but doubted whether, without an element of surprise, anyone could defeat a skilled swordsman by relying on spirit alone

"Try to strike me," Shōju then challenged. That was the invitation the swordsmen were waiting for, and they leaped at Shōju. Not one of them was able to hit him, however, but they all received at least one good rap on the head with his fan. Thoroughly humbled, they asked him his secret.

"If your eye is true and your mind unobstructed, there is nothing you cannot overcome, including a sword attack," Shōju informed them. (Hakuin was to learn well from Shōju, for he displayed a similar presence of mind when confronted by a skeptical samurai later in his career.)

At his first interview with Shōju, Hakuin presented the formidable old fellow with a well-composed "poem of enlightenment." Without giving it a glance, Shōju crumpled the paper in his left hand, threatened Hakuin with his right fist, and demanded to know, "Other than a smattering of book learning, what have you attained?"

"If I had something to show you, I'd spit it out!" Hakuin responded.

The master then asked sharply, "How about *Mu?*"

"No hand or foot can touch it," Hakuin replied confidently.

Shōju suddenly reached out, tweaked Hakuin's nose hard, and shouted, "Here's a place to put my hands and feet!"

Mortified, Hakuin realized that his previous enlightenment was incomplete. Shōju then gave Hakuin another *kōan* to ponder: "Where did Zen master Nan-ch'üan [Nansen, 748–834] go when he died?"

Hakuin later came to Shōju with a verse in answer, but the master shouted, "Delusion and pure fantasy!" and rained so many blows on Hakuin that he was knocked off the veranda.

The despondent Hakuin could not solve this *kōan* or any others Shōju put to him. Totally discouraged, Hakuin used his customary tactic when faced with an impasse: he made a vow. "If I fail to master one of these *kōan* in seven days, I'll kill myself."

Shōju was far from impressed, however, and continued to heap abuse on his bewildered student, whom he called "a half-wit monk stuck in a dark, putrid cave of demons."

Appalled, Hakuin asked, "Why am I listening to this country bumpkin in this shack of a temple? This country is full of outstanding masters—there must be someone better for me."

"Go ahead and scour the world for a better teacher," Shōju jeered. "You'll be more likely to see the stars at noon."

Utterly confused, as Hakuin set off on his begging rounds the next morning he was preoccupied with his life-or-death problems. Standing before the gate of one house in a kind of trance, he was oblivious to the shouts of "Go away! We have nothing to give!" emanating from within. Subsequently, the old woman who lived there was so irritated by his apparent persistence that she rushed out and beat him over the head with a bamboo broom. Hakuin was knocked unconscious, but when he came to, the solutions to all the *kōan* he had been agonizing over had become crystal clear. He jumped up and cried out in joy, much to the surprise of the villagers who had gathered around the prostrate monk. "The old crone must have beaten his senses out," they agreed. "Better stay away from this crazy monk." Years later, Hakuin was to commemorate this momentous event in a painting of a bamboo broom with the inscrip-

tion, "This is the broom that sweeps away cheap enlightenments!"

Although the normally dour Shōju smiled when Hakuin
recounted the day's dramatic events, he gave no formal confir-
mation of Hakuin's enlightenment, perhaps because he knew
that Hakuin would reach even higher levels. That night,
Hakuin's mother appeared to Hakuin in a dream with the wel-
come news that she was no longer wandering in limbo. The
great merit accrued from her son's quest and enlightenment
had been transferred to her, and she was now resting comfort-
ably in heaven. (Such "merit-transference" was an important
element of Japanese Buddhism, and many people became
monks or nuns to effect the salvation of a deceased loved one.)

Although Hakuin had been with Shōju only eight months,
he was now certain that he was on the right path. The twenty-
two-year-old Hakuin returned to Shōin-ji at the end of 1708
and never saw Shōju (who died in 1721) again, though he
always considered Shōju his "root master." Shōju's death verse
was:

> My final verse:
> Die quickly is hard to say.
> Speak with wordless words,
> But do not talk, do not talk!

After a brief stay at Shōin-ji, Hakuin set out again at the
beginning of 1709. Each time he grasped the essence of one of
the thousands of *kōan* he had memorized, he would dance
about and laugh deliriously, behavior that earned him a reputation as a "Zen madman." After experiencing a series of large
and small enlightenments, the constant excitement unhinged
Hakuin and he fell seriously ill with what he termed "Zen sickness." The alarming symptoms were:

> Burning fevers and splitting headaches; a lower
> back that feels as if it is wrapped in ice; watery
> eyes; ringing in the ears; dread of nature when in

the sunlight; deep depression when in the dark; troubled thoughts during the day; bad dreams at night; listlessness; exhaustion; poor digestion; and terrible chills.

Fortunately, during the next two years, Hakuin was able to cure himself of this dreadful ailment and continue his demanding training.

At the end of 1711, Hakuin returned to Daishō-ji to care for Sokudō, another of his former teachers who had fallen ill. As before, Hakuin spent the day tending his master and the night in *zazen*. The next year, Hakuin, aged twenty-six, began giving public lectures at Shōin-ji. When Sokudō died that fall, Hakuin set off once more on a pilgrimage. In an incident typical of his days on the road, Hakuin suddenly became enlightened about the meaning of the *kōan*, "Lotus leaves rounder than the roundest mirror; water chestnut spines sharper than the sharpest drill." It was pouring with rain at the time, and the elated monk fell over and rolled in the mud laughing hysterically.

Another time, Hakuin was doing *zazen* at night when the sound of softly falling snow triggered his comprehension of the *kōan*, "A young girl's power of meditation surpasses that of the Buddha's wisest disciple." He composed a poem to mark this awakening:

If only I could share it:
The soft sound of snow
Falling late at night
From the trees
At this old temple.

In 1713, Hakuin headed south to meet Kōgetsu (1667–1751), reputed to be the leading Zen master of the day, but he got sidetracked and passed the year training with the masters Tetsudō (1658–1730) and Egoku (1632–1721). Despite his earlier brush with death from "Zen sickness," Hakuin was as hard on himself as ever. He and another monk once did a seven-day retreat of continuous *zazen*, sitting facing each other with a cudgel between them. If either showed signs of dozing off, the other was to rap him between the eyes with the cudgel. They completed the retreat without resorting to the club once.

In 1714, Hakuin trained at Reishō-ji and then spent the next two years in retreat at Mount Iwataki. He had unwisely resumed this severe bout of training too soon, and his health deteriorated again. To recuperate, he lived quietly in a charming hermitage among the beautiful Iwataki mountains, subsisting on rice gruel and meditating day and night. The reverie was broken in 1716, when a servant of his father finally tracked him down after a two-year search. "Your father is ill and Shōin-ji is empty and has fallen into ruin," the servant reported. "We want you to come home."

Consequently, in the first month of 1717, the thirty-one-year-old Hakuin installed himself as abbot of Shōin-ji, now little more than an abandoned shell. Hakuin began the painstaking process of rebuilding the temple and establishing it as a training center. His father died at the end of that year.

The next year, Hakuin was honored with an invitation to serve as the head monk for the winter training period at Myōshin-ji in Kyoto, one of the largest and most important Zen monasteries in the country. This could have been the first step to fame and wealth as a Zen master in the capital, but he returned to Shōin-ji as soon as the three-month session was over, determined to pass the rest of his days as abbot of that little rural temple. This is alluded to in the name "Hakuin," which he adopted around this time (as a youth he was called Iwajirō and his initial monastic name was Ekaku). "*Hakuin*" means "concealed in white," referring to the state of being hidden in the clouds and snow of Mount Fuji (in other words, one with Buddha-nature), being lost in training in the remote White Crane Valley of Shōin-ji, and being absorbed in the whiteness of nirvana, in which all things find peace.

Over the next decade, a small number of trainee monks and lay followers began to gather at Shōin-ji to practice Zen under Hakuin's direction. His reputation was greatly enhanced after an incident when he was accused by a local girl of fathering her illegitimate child. Hakuin said nothing in his defense, and when the girl's outraged father demanded that he raise the child, Hakuin took the infant in. He gently cared for the baby without complaint, arranged for a wet nurse, and took it along on begging trips with him, silently enduring the scorn heaped on him by the villagers. Eventually the girl was stricken with remorse and confessed the truth—a young neighbor was the father, not Hakuin. The girl's mortified father begged forgiveness, but Hakuin replied calmly, "Don't worry about it," and handed the baby back, never mentioning the incident again.

One night in 1725, Hakuin had another vision of his mother in a dream, this time presenting her son with a purple robe. The robe had mirrors on both sleeves, mirrors that reflected the inner and outer dimensions of life with great splendor while sparkling with the serenity of nirvana, thus giving Hakuin the key to the *kōan*, "The enlightened one sees Buddha-nature with his own eyes."

The next year, Hakuin, aged forty, was poring over the *Lotus Sutra*, a text he had largely considered worthless, when a cricket chirped softly. Hakuin suddenly understood the underlying message of the text—"Outside the mind there is no *Lotus Sutra*; outside the *Lotus Sutra* there is no mind"—and now agreed that the work deserved to be called the "King of Buddhist texts."

Hakuin's earliest biographers described this event as the turning point of his life. The quest for enlightenment that consumed the first half of Hakuin's career was the "seed" of his practice, characterized by a near-obsession with the problems of self—avoiding hell, experiencing enlightenment, maintaining physical and mental health. With Hakuin's maturity, the latter half of his career as a Zen master was the "fruit"—selfless devotion to the care and nourishment of others.

Unlike Ikkyū, who had many students but refused to designate anyone as his successor, or Ryōkan, who never served as an abbot of a temple and died without a single disciple, Hakuin was the "Master Teacher" of Japanese Zen. Hundreds of monastic and lay trainees studied under his guidance, and he seems to have certified, or otherwise sanctioned, more than eighty of his direct disciples to teach and promote Hakuin-style Zen throughout the country. He probably presented more *inka*—to monks, nuns, laymen and -women, and even to one couple— than any other Zen master in Japanese history. All of the present-day major Rinzai sects trace their lineage to Hakuin and still largely follow his teaching style.

Hakuin-style Zen was based on his lengthy quest and his forceful character—"Our master moved like a bull and glared like a tiger," one of his disciples wrote in awe. "Never be satisfied with small attainments," Hakuin urged his students. He insisted that his trainees confront, suffer through, and surmount the same massive barriers that he encountered. A real student needs great doubt, he was convinced: "If one's doubt measures ten degrees in intensity, so will one's enlightenment."

Hakuin demanded that his disciples grapple with ultimate questions by chewing on, swallowing, and spitting out the *kōan* he himself had butted his head against and by tackling the *kōan* of his own invention: "What is the sound of one hand clapping?" The sole purpose of Zen training, declared Hakuin, is *kenshō*, "seeing into your nature," thereby becoming the Buddha.

Like Daitō and Ikkyū, whom he greatly admired, Hakuin tirelessly denounced adherents of "Silent-Illumination" and "Do-Nothing" (that is, "Unborn" or "Ordinary") Zen. "Silent-Illumination" was the main emphasis of one faction of the Sōtō Zen school, which eschewed the use of *kōan* in favor of "sitting like the Buddha" and equated the act of *zazen* with enlightenment. The apologists of "Silent-Illumination" Zen contended that enlightenment occurred naturally and only once, and talk of "eighteen great enlightenments and uncountable minor ones" was nothing more than excessive emotionalism, not true awakening. Hakuin countered that in addition to his own experience there were dozens of examples of multiple enlightenments in Zen literature. Furthermore, he had often attempted "Silent-Illumination" Zen as a young monk but found himself in a state of continual depression and apathy.

Hakuin had an even stronger aversion to "Do-Nothing" Zen. This stream of Zen devolved from Bankei (1622–53), a monk who had undergone asceticism as extreme as Hakuin's and experienced a similarly profound awakening, but who had come to the opposite conclusion: that intense training had been useless and kept leading him astray. Artificial methods such as forcing oneself to sit endlessly in *zazen*, spending months trying to solve senseless riddles, and storming monasteries to challenge the masters were futile, he decided. One's Buddhahood is innate and irrevocable—unborn: "There is not one instant, awake or asleep, when you are not a Buddha," Bankei taught, and hence there was no need to goad or bully students into seeking *kenshō*. While Bankei manifested a high degree of attainment, his followers took him literally, and Hakuin complained that in temples headed by teachers of the "Do-Nothing" Zen school, the practitioners were sitting like bumps on a log, nodding off and accomplishing nothing. He accused them of giving up on Zen and trivializing the great struggles of the Buddha and Bodhidharma. Such priests were no better than thieves, Hakuin charged, sponging off their parishioners without providing anything in return. For instance, Hakuin said his immediate predecessor at Shōin-ji had applied that heretical teaching of "Do-Nothing" Zen to the temple itself, letting the

---

Self-portrait of Hakuin at the Age of Seventy-one. (Shōin-ji Treasury, Japan)
Hakuin is showing his stern side here, "glaring like a tiger and moving like a bull," and he appears ready to apply his stick to any lazy monks that may appear. Other self-portraits are drawn with less restraint, with Hakuin depicting himself as a cross-eyed dunce, a cagy old monk, or a gentle grandpa. The lengthy inscriptions are by Hakuin's disciple Tōrei, and the calligraphy above his master's head reproduces a verse often used by Hakuin to describe himself:

> Among an assembly of Buddhas,
>   all Buddhas dislike him.
> In a congregation of demons,
>   all demons detest him,
> This decrepit old baldy
>   who appears here again on paper!

roof leak, the walls crumble, and the floor rot! Hakuin-style Zen eventually prevailed over "Do-Nothing" Zen, which disappeared within a few generations of Bankei's death.

Hakuin's motto was: "Meditation in the midst of action is a billion times superior to meditation in stillness." Hakuin's master Shōju once told him: "If you can maintain your presence of mind in a city street teeming with violent activity, in a cremation ground amid death and destruction, and in a theater surrounded by noise and distraction, then, and only then, are you a true practitioner of Zen."

Similarly, Hakuin wrote in one of his essays:

> Rather than shutting yourself in a room to guard your gold, you should be out in the street sharing your wealth with others. . . . What would happen to this world if lords and ministers, warriors, merchants, craftsmen, and farmers all shirked their duties and went off somewhere to practice blindly sitting and silent illumination in the vain hope of avoiding difficulties and slipping trouble-free through life? Society would collapse!

He cited the example of sages who expressed their Zen by humping stones, tilling the earth, fetching water, chopping wood, growing vegetables, measuring and making, spinning and weaving, studying and teaching, governing and protecting.

The Chinese abbot Pai-chang (Hyakujō, 749–814) was out laboring in the fields well into his nineties, Hakuin noted, and when his disciples hid his tools in an attempt to get him to rest, Pai-chang refused to eat: "No work, no food!" Hakuin also held up the examples of many outstanding laymen and -women who had lived in the outside world, yet never separated themselves from the Way of Zen. "Make everything in your life a *kōan*," Hakuin urged his students, lay and monastic alike. "Think of the mountains, rivers, and the great Earth as your meditation platform, and the universe as your personal meditation cave." The wisdom attained by practicing Zen in the midst of the world of desire is unshakable, Hakuin taught, "like a lotus flower that can never be destroyed." He also stated, "A valiant practitioner, behaving like a warrior beset by enemies on all sides, can attain enlightenment in an instant, but those who dillydally will take three eons to wake up."

Hakuin's teaching is summed up in his most popular work, *The Song of Meditation (Zazen wasan)*:

> Sentient beings are originally Buddhas,
> Like water and ice.
> There is no ice without water,
> No Buddhas outside sentient beings.
> Yet sentient beings don't know how close it is,
> And search for it far away. How sad!
> It's like dying of thirst
> In the middle of a fount of water;
> Or a rich man's son
> Wandering like a lost beggar.
> We are bound to the realm of *samsara*
> Because ignorance keeps us in darkness.
> Walking in darkness,
> When will we escape from birth and death?
> The Zen of the Great Vehicle
> Is beyond all superlatives.
> Charity, precepts, all the other virtues,
> Chanting, repentance, training, and
> All good works
> Have their source in Zen.
> Sit sincerely in meditation just once,
> And it erases layers of evil karma.
> No longer in the valley of hell,
> The Pure Land is so close.
> Reverently listen to this teaching
> Just one time,
> Praise and rejoice in it,
> And boundless good fortune will be yours.
> Better yet, dedicate yourself

Directly to enlightening your own nature;
Once self-nature equals no nature,
You'll be free of this empty chatter.
Open the gate of cause and effect
And walk straight ahead without delay.
Use no-form as form,
Wander without settling down.
Use no-thought as thought,
Sing and dance with the Buddha's Law.
Open the vastness of unobstructed repose,
Bask in the brilliance of complete wisdom.
At this very moment, what do we need to seek?
Nirvana is before our eyes.
This place is the Lotus Land,
This body is that of the Buddha.

Although Hakuin was a curmudgeon in his writings, blasting his Zen rivals and belittling other schools of Buddhism—"Zen is for giants, the Pure Land for midgets"—he was, in fact, an extraordinarily wise and gentle Zen master and catholic Buddhist who never turned people away because of their beliefs and who incorporated elements of all religions into his teaching.

His knowledge is incomparably vast, and it is said that he has read through the entire Buddhist canon seven times. He presents every student with a *kōan* to ponder, but he does it according to the school that the person follows, posing a question taken from the appropriate tradition—Zen, Tendai, Shingon, Pure Land, Nichiren, Taoist, Confucian, Shintoist.

To Hakuin, Zen's "See into your nature and become the Buddha" was equivalent to the "One thought, three thousand worlds" of Tendai, the "Mystical letter A" of Shingon, the "Rebirth" of the Pure Land schools, the "Wondrous Law" of

Nichiren, the "Way" of the Taoists, the "Ultimate Good" of the Confucians, and the "High Plain of Heaven" of the Shintoists.

A lot of Hakuin's bad-mouthing of other sects and teachers was actually good-natured ribbing. One of Hakuin's friends was Tenkei (1648–1735), a Sōtō Zen master. Once, when on a journey, Hakuin was in Tenkei's neighborhood and asked a passerby, "Does a chap named Tenkei live nearby?"

"Yes," the man replied with some irritation. "Around here, Zen Master Tenkei is considered a living Buddha."

"Is that so? Well, next time you see him, tell him that I said he was a worthless fool!"

The man was shocked by such language, but Hakuin escaped before he could be forced to retract it.

The man happened to be a dedicated follower of Tenkei and reported the incident to his master. Tenkei said with a laugh, "So old Hakuin is back in town. Sounds like he is in fine fettle. Thank you for the message."

Hakuin's grim do-or-die *kenshō* Zen was balanced by his insistence that Zen training must include fits of ecstatic, blissful laughter; the deeper the *kenshō*, the more one overflows with side-splitting mirth. He also said, "Those who understand jokes are many; those who understand true laughter are few." As we shall see, this essential element of humor is most evident in Hakuin's Zen cartoons.

Hakuin could appreciate humor even when he was the butt of the joke. One day the wealthiest family in the district invited Hakuin to a feast of vegetarian dishes. Hakuin, clad in his simple black robe and wearing straw sandals, made his way to their mansion on foot, but when it was time to leave his hosts insisted that he be carried back by palanquin. However, as soon as the bearers picked up the palanquin to set off, Hakuin, who had never ridden in such a fancy vehicle before, tumbled to the ground, much to the amusement of the crowd seeing him off.

"Enough of that," said Hakuin with a smile. "I should have followed my own advice—always keep your feet on the ground!"

Among Hakuin's numerous followers were scores of women, some of them from the pleasure quarters in Hara, but he treated his female disciples no differently from laymen or monks. One of Hakuin's first disciples was a fifteen-year-old girl named Satsu, who was having trouble attracting suitors because of her plainness, so her parents instructed her to pray to Kannon for a suitable mate. One day her father was shocked to see her sitting on a copy of the *Kannon Sutra*.

"What are you doing sitting on that holy book?" he exclaimed angrily.

"What's the matter?" asked Satsu coolly. "The priest at Shōin-ji said everything has Buddha-nature, so how can there be a difference between my rear end and a sutra?"

Completely nonplussed, the father consulted Hakuin, who said with a smile, "Your daughter is pretty sharp. Give her this *kōan* poem and tell her it's from me":

> In the night's darkness,
> If you can hear the voice
> Of the crow that does not cry,
> The unborn future will be clear
> And you can understand your father's love.

When shown the verse, Satsu was not impressed.

"What's so clever about that? Hakuin is not a whit better than I!"

When Satsu came later to see Hakuin, he greeted her with this *kōan*: "Have you grasped all of space?"

In reply, Satsu described a circle in the air with her finger.

"That's only half the picture," Hakuin replied with a glare.

"Too late. I've already finished grasping it!"

Satsu was a real handful. During an interview she once asked Hakuin to elucidate a difficult point. As soon as he began to speak, Satsu said, "Thank you," leaving the master with his mouth agape.

An arrogant monk once tried to get the better of Satsu: "Within a rubbish heap a white rock is smashed; what is the principle of this?"

Without a moment's hesitation, Satsu smashed the monk's teacup to bits, and he beat a hasty retreat.

Satsu resisted attempts to marry her off since she wanted to continue to practice *zazen* full-time, but Hakuin told her, "You comprehend Zen well, but you need to put it into practice. It is best for you to marry, acting in accordance with the natural pairing of male and female. Spirit and form, enlightenment and actualization must be harmonized with the realities of everyday life." In other words, marrying, having sex, and bearing and raising children were excellent forms of moving meditation.

Satsu followed her master's advice, wed, and had a big family. Years later, after losing one of her beloved grandchildren, Satsu was inconsolable. A callous neighbor remarked to her, "I heard that you received a certificate of enlightenment from Hakuin himself, so why are you carrying on so?"

"Idiot!" Satsu shot back. "My tears are a better memorial than a hundred priests chanting lugubriously. The tears commemorate every child that has died. That is exactly how I feel at this moment!"

Ōhashi, another of Hakuin's disciples, managed to achieve enlightenment even while serving as a pleasure girl. A lovely, talented young woman, Ōhashi indentured herself to a Hara brothel to support her family when her samurai father lost his position on the death of his lord. She studied Zen with Hakuin, who advised her to contemplate life as the ultimate *kōan*— enlightenment was possible in any circumstance.

Although terrified by thunder, one day Ōhashi made herself sit on the veranda during a violent storm in order to rid herself of her fear. A bolt of lightning hit the ground in front of her, knocking her unconscious. When she came to, she felt as if the universe were hers. Hakuin certified her *kenshō*, thereby showing that even a courtesan could become enlightened. Ōhashi was eventually redeemed by a rich patron, whom she wed. Later, with her husband's permission, she became a nun renowned for her wisdom and compassion. On her death. instead of making the customary memorial tablet, her husband and friends had Ōhashi carved as Kannon, Goddess of Com-

passion, and had the image placed within Hakuin's temple.

Hakuin was very understanding of human nature. Once a lord was traveling and stopped off in Hara, only to fall desperately in love with an innkeeper's daughter. Despite the promise of undying love and wealth, the girl refused to leave her aged parents. Hakuin carved a little wooden image of the girl for the lord to keep by his side in the hope that she would one day consent to join him. (Unfortunately, the girl died shortly thereafter, and the lord had to be content with memories of his beloved.)

On the other hand, Hakuin was furious when a high-ranking samurai showed up with his "younger sister"—in other words, his mistress—in tow. When the samurai came for an interview, Hakuin scolded him severely: "Zen training demands that you be sincere from the crown of your head to the soles of your feet! Even the smallest lie negates years of training." The samurai immediately saw the error of his ways and introduced his concubine to Hakuin. Both of them eventually became fine Zen students.

"Zen grannies," shrewd old women who love to confound pompous monks, are a frequent occurrence in Zen literature, and Hakuin had run-ins with a few himself. "Old San," one such lady, couldn't wait to test Hakuin when he visited her home town. In the interview, Hakuin held up one hand, silently challenging her to hear its sound. She yelled, "Better than listening to Hakuin's 'one hand,' let's clap both and do some real business."

Dragon Staff and Fly Whisk, by Hakuin. (Genshin Collection, U.S.A.)
This is an example of the *inka*, or "Zen diplomas," that Hakuin presented to his disciples. The dragon staff and fly whisk symbolize the enlightenment and teaching authority of Zen. The inscription reads:

> Autumn (1758). The layman Sugizaki Jakuzen, of Shirako in Ise Province, shattered heavy barriers by hearing "The Sound of One Hand." Therefore, I have brushed this as proof of his attainment. Is not one who has staked all for this great prize truly a valiant warrior?

Hakuin shot back, "If you can do business by clapping both hands, then there's no need to hear the sound of one," and he grabbed a piece of paper and brushed a painting of a bamboo broom on it. He passed it to Old San for an inscription. She wrote:

> This broom
> Sweeps away
> All the imposters in Japan—
> First of all
> Hakuin of Hara!

This confrontation itself has became a *kōan*: "Who won? Hakuin or Old San?"

Then there was the old lady in Hara who heard Hakuin say in a lecture, "Your mind is the Pure Land, your body is that of Amida Buddha."

This served as her *kōan*, and one morning she experienced *kenshō* while cleaning up after breakfast. She rushed over to Shōin-ji and announced to Hakuin, "Amida has engulfed my body! The universe radiates! How truly marvelous!"

"Nonsense!" Hakuin retorted. "Does it shine up your asshole?"

The tiny old woman gave the large Hakuin a shove and shouted, "What do you know about enlightenment?"

Then they both roared with laughter.

Another anecdote tells of a layman named Harushige who lost his oldest son to illness, squandered his inheritance on wine and women, and despaired of life. One day, he came across a book that contained the line Hakuin loved to quote: "A valiant practitioner . . . can attain enlightenment in an instant, but those who dillydally will take three eons to wake up." He shut himself in his bathhouse, vowing to achieve understanding or die. On the third straight day of sitting, racked with pain and suffering from hallucinations, Harushige suddenly had a breakthrough. Hakuin confirmed Harushige's *kenshō*, and frequently mentioned him as an example of one who attained great things by risking all on *kōan* Zen. Hakuin continued to guide Haru-shige, who was transformed into a hard-working family man, a friend to the poor, a builder of roads and bridges, and a pillar of the community.

One troubled young widow became so obsessed with her *kōan* study that she spent all her time sitting in the meditation hall at Shōin-ji. Fortunately, her neighbors made meals for her son in the woman's absence, but when she briefly returned home she said to him, "Who are you?"

"I'm your son! Have you forgotten me?" the son replied.

Even Hakuin thought such singlemindedness excessive and told her to resolve her *kōan* without further delay. She did so, Hakuin approved, and the woman resumed a more normal existence. (An abbot friend of Hakuin met her once and remarked, "In all my years I have never seen a person so absorbed in Zen training as that woman.")

One day Hakuin was walking in the temple garden with a lay disciple who had been puzzling over the meaning of the character for "death," which had been given to him as a *kōan*. Offering him a different approach, Hakuin recited a poem:

> Mount Sumeru,
> The Cosmic Peak,
> Collapses;
> Heaven is shattered
> Into bits and pieces!

"Understand?" Hakuin inquired hopefully. The lay disciple, as if suddenly released from a great burden, picked up a small stone and tossed it high in the sky. Hakuin smiled in approval.

Once, a pawnbroker's son visited Hakuin and told the master of his plight: "I want my father to practice Buddhism, but he says that he is too busy with his account books to spare even a few seconds to do a single *nenbutsu* [the chanting of Amida Buddha's name]."

Hakuin knew that the pawnbroker was a miser and that this was just an excuse to avoid religion altogether. He told the son,

"Tell your father that I will buy his *nenbutsu*—one penny for each recitation."

The stingy pawnbroker was overjoyed that he could actually make a profit from religion. Each day he presented Hakuin with his bill for the *nenbutsu* and the master duly paid. By the seventh day of the contract, however, the pawnbroker became so absorbed in the chanting that he forgot to count. He soon became so devoted to the *nenbutsu* that he recited it free of charge and eventually became a generous patron of Hakuin's temple.

On occasion, people would challenge Hakuin in public, shouting out *kōan* during his public lectures. Once someone in the audience demanded to know, "After death, do we disappear or continue?" Hakuin responded, "Right now, are you disappearing or continuing?"

Hakuin posed a similar *kōan* to a senior monk who came for instruction: "Where did you come from at birth and where will you go at death?"

It took the elder monk a year to come up with an answer. When Hakuin repeated the *kōan*, the monk held up one finger.

"That's not good enough! Tell me more!" demanded Hakuin with a scowl.

The monk replied, "Where did *you* come from at birth and where will *you* go at death?"

This time Hakuin approved.

One samurai wished to know, "What is heaven? What is hell?"

"What's the matter? Are you frightened of hell?" Hakuin sneered. "A sniveling coward like you is not worth teaching!"

Incensed by Hakuin's insults, the samurai drew his sword and chased Hakuin into the main hall. He struck with blind fury at the master, who suddenly disappeared into the shadows.

"This anger is your hell," Hakuin yelled.

The samurai calmed down and apologized for losing his temper.

"That's heaven," Hakuin said to him. (Since a samurai had to be perpetually on guard, always properly dressed, and ready to lay down his life at any time, Hakuin once wrote that an accomplished samurai could accomplish in one month what it takes an untroubled monk a year to do.)

Since Hara was an important post-station on the Tōkaidō Highway, provincial lords making the obligatory biannual visits to Edo used to stop there, and a number of them became Hakuin's students. Hakuin would serve the lords the simple millet cakes the farmers gave him, and if a pampered lord turned up his nose at such coarse fare he would get a scathing lecture from Hakuin on the virtues of plain living and simple food.

Once the wealthiest lord of southern Japan stopped at Hara and complained of a stomach ailment to Hakuin. "I can cure it," Hakuin assured him. "Don't eat breakfast tomorrow and come straight here."

The lord showed up early the next day and Hakuin informed him, "This cure is secret, so you must follow my instructions exactly. You can drink this tea, but then you must stay in this room until I return."

Hakuin left the lord alone. By noon the lord was starving. Around three o'clock in the afternoon Hakuin entered the room with a small bowl.

"Sorry," Hakuin apologized. "It took longer than expected to prepare the medicine. Here it is."

"What is this?" the lord asked, taking the bowl.

"Gruel of wheat and a little rice and two pickles made with daikon," Hakuin told him. The lord had never seen such food before but, seasoned with hunger, it tasted delicious.

"I hope that you have taken the cure," Hakuin said. "When the crops fail, the farmers in your domain experience the kind of hunger you felt. Never forget how that feels when they ask for help. Gruel and pickles are what they eat, and it is better for you than the rich food you stuff yourself with."

Hakuin never tired of reminding each samurai lord who visited him that farmers were the treasures of the nation and they deserved to be treated well. In his letters, essays, and paintings, he instructed the lords always to be benevolent, frugal, and temperate—"treat the people with kindness and the root of the nation will flourish; abuse them and the country will be ruined."

This Zen master practiced what he preached. Hakuin lived as simply as a peasant himself. During the first lean years of his tenure at Shōin-ji, Hakuin's soup was not infrequently seasoned with maggots since the temple only had spoiled soybean paste discarded by farmers. Once a wealthy lord offered to provide Hakuin with anything he needed. "Well, we broke one of our kitchen bowls this morning, and we would be grateful for a replacement," Hakuin told him. When the lord returned to his domain in Bizen, a district famed for its pottery, he had a number of fine bowls made for Hakuin's temple. Hakuin displayed one of the beautiful bowls by hanging it upside down on a branch of a pine tree in the temple garden. The bowl is still there now, hanging high in the air.

When conditions improved at Shōin-ji, Hakuin stored foodstuffs and grain at the temple for use in times of famine. He also planted hundreds of trees along the banks of the river to prevent floods, painstakingly experimenting until he found which seedlings took root the best. (Hakuin was apparently a keen botanist, for he titled a number of his essays with the names of weeds—"Goose Grass," "Horse Thistles," "Snake Strawberries," "Wild Ivy"—and a number of his paintings include exotic plants.)

One bitterly cold winter day, a lord visited Shōin-ji and Hakuin thoughtfully had some saké warmed for him. While they were chatting, Hakuin noticed the lord's spear bearer shivering in the entrance hall. "Why don't you give your guard a cup of this hot saké? The poor fellow is freezing to death." The next time the lord and his entourage were in Hara, the guard, now a full-fledged samurai, called on Hakuin to thank him. "In our domain, if the lord presents a soldier with a cup of saké he is thereby elevated to the status of a samurai [a custom of which Hakuin was well aware]. I'll be for ever grateful to you."

Hakuin warned the lords against addiction to sex and the costly habit of surrounding themselves with vain and frivolous women. He decried the common practice of squandering small fortunes to secure the services of courtesans from Kyoto, girls who were soon discarded or exchanged for others, and expressed outrage that as much as one-third of a domain's budget would go to procure and maintain a bevy of concubines.

Two of Hakuin's top disciples were Tōrei (1721–92) and Suiō (1717–89). Tōrei had been born into a merchant's family, and as a child he was serious and thoughtful, and refused to harm even lice. He was a prodigy much like Hakuin, and when he was five years old the famous Zen master Kōgetsu stayed at his home. The little boy was so impressed by Kōgetsu's gentle demeanor that he decided then and there that he wanted to emulate him. His parents did everything to dissuade him, but Tōrei finally obtained their permission and was ordained a Zen novice at the age of nine. He trained with Kōgetsu in Kyūshū for some years, and then, at the age of twenty-two, began a difficult period of training under Hakuin, whom he had met in Kyoto. He fell seriously ill, however, perhaps with "Zen sickness," and hovered near death; upon his recovery, he gave Hakuin an account of the insights he gained from the experience and was shortly thereafter presented with an *inka*.

Tōrei served as Hakuin's right-hand man for many years and became his principal heir. He served as abbot of the two temples Hakuin founded, Muryō-ji in 1752 (which did not survive the Buddhist persecutions of the nineteenth century) and Ryūtaku-ji in 1760 (which flourishes to this day as an international Zen training center). It was Tōrei who compiled the first biography of Hakuin, and it was he who systematically organized the *kōan* of Hakuin-style Zen. Tōrei was as strict, meticulous, and persevering as his master and nearly as good a scholar. He was devoted to harmonizing the Three Great Teachings and stated, "Shintō is the root, Confucianism is the trunk and leaves, and Buddhism is the flowering and sweet fruit."

Suiō, on the other hand, was a free spirit who could not have been more different from Tōrei (or Hakuin). No one knew where he really came from—rumor had it that he was the bastard son of a lord and a courtesan. Even after becoming Hakuin's disciple at the age of thirty, Suiō enjoyed the company of women and the taste of saké. Suiō had no use for *zazen* or ceremony, and only went to Shōin-ji to hear Hakuin lecture. As soon as Hakuin's talk was over, Suiō would return to his little hut, not bothering to be interviewed by his teacher. Occasionally, Hakuin would send his attendants after Suiō, but to no avail. Despite Suiō's dislike of temple life and his total disregard of rules and regulations, Hakuin had a high opinion of his Zen ability and designated Suiō his successor at Shōin-ji when he retired at the age of eighty. The two had a temporary falling out, which pained Hakuin deeply, but Suiō eventually returned as abbot of Shōin-ji and was with Hakuin when he died. Later, Suiō was buried next to his master. The fierce Hakuin must have had a very big heart to love the wayward Suiō so much. And Suiō faithfully carried on the Hakuin tradition of using wonderful paintings to spread the Zen message. During his lifetime, Suiō directed most students to train with Tōrei, who was the abbot of Ryūtaku-ji.

Interestingly, there is a *kōan* featuring Suiō and Tōrei that is sometimes still used in Rinzai Zen training. Suiō said to Tōrei, "These days everybody and his brother are babbling about 'Hearing the sound of one hand.' But what do you think they *really* heard?" The *kōan* is: "What did Tōrei say in reply?"

Gasan (1727–97), Hakuin's last monastic disciple, came to Hakuin when the master was in his eighties. He was a brash fellow who had studied with over thirty Zen masters; he wrote that he was not cowed by Hakuin's reputation in the least, nor was he intimidated by the fact that Hakuin had more than eight hundred students. "I challenged him three times and three times he vanquished me. I was awestruck." Gasan was the teacher of Inzan (1754–1817) and Takujū (1760–1833), from whom all the present principal Rinzai Zen schools are descended.

Although it never had the impact of the Hakuin school, mention must be made of the Kōgetsu line of Zen. Many of Hakuin's monastic disciples (including Tōrei) started their training under Kōgetsu, coming to Shōin-ji after that master retired, so there was a great deal of cross-fertilization between the styles—Ryōsai (1706–86), for example, the first person to be presented with an *inka* by Hakuin, later returned to Kōgetsu, and was fortunate to benefit from the wisdom of both masters.

Kōgetsu was born in 1667, so he was nineteen years Hakuin's senior. He had become a Zen novice at the age of ten, but the first abbot he served was a drunkard, and the young monk had his hands full just caring for him, with no hope of any instruction in the classics. One night after putting the intoxicated abbot to bed, Kōgetsu met a leper cringing at the back of the temple. Kōgetsu learned that the poor fellow had once been the chief instructor of the main educational institution in the domain but had lost his position when he contracted the disease. Kōgetsu built a shelter for the leper and brought him three meals a day in exchange for lessons.

Kōgetsu went on to become the top Zen scholar of his day, and he also spent years on pilgrimages studying with virtually every Zen master in the land (including Bankei). Like Hakuin, he spurned offers of high positions in the monasteries of Kyoto and spent the last fifty years of his life in distant Kyūshū, studying and teaching. The Kōgetsu tradition of Zen was gentler, quieter, and more refined than that of Hakuin. Sengai (1750–1837), Hakuin's only rival as a Zen artist, belonged to the Kōgetsu line, ensuring that this tradition of Zen will live for ever in the wonderful brushstrokes of his paintings.

Training in Hakuin-style Zen required great stamina, and "Zen health" was an important element of his teaching. Quoting the medical classics of China, Hakuin instructed his disciples:

> The key to nourishing life is to strengthen the body. The secret of strengthening the body lies in concentrating the spirit. When the spirit is concentrated, energy develops. When energy develops, the elixir of life is forged. When the elixir of life is forged, the body becomes steadfast. When the body is steadfast, the spirit is perfected. . . . The elixir of life, the "vital breath," is forged and concentrated in the *tan*, a spot two

inches beneath the navel. As it develops, that
area should become pendulous and well-round-
ed, a reservoir of energy and health.

Hakuin followed this method, and boasted that he had ten times
the vitality at seventy that he had at thirty. Without suffering
from fatigue, he could sit in *zazen* all day, chant sutras from
morning to night, and speak or write for hours.

Still, many of his disciples fell ill, some with the "Zen sickness" that had once devastated Hakuin. The young Hakuin was
a clearly manic-depressive, and his malady would today be
diagnosed as a nervous breakdown. The method that Hakuin
devised to treat the condition was called *naikan*, "introspec-
tion." Hakuin described *naikan* in his book *Evening Chat on a
Boat (Yasen kanna)*, and, in fact, *naikan* therapy has been
adopted by certain modern psychiatrists both in Japan and the
West. Although Hakuin reportedly learned *naikan* from a mys-
terious hermit of great age called Hakuyū, modern research
indicates that he compiled the methods in *Evening Chat* from a
variety of sources and his own extensive experiences and
experiments with mind-healing.

To cure the dreaded ailment, Hakuin prescribed (in addition
to the pill of "seeing into one's nature and becoming the Buddha," the best medicine there is) this treatment:

Imagine a duck egg–sized lump of the sweetest,
most fragrant cream on the crown of your head.
Let it melt gradually downward through your
body, filling every pore, flushing out all sickness
and disease as it spreads to the soles of your feet.
As the warm cream circulates back up through
the body, the internal organs are purified, the
skin becomes radiant, and the equilibrium of
body and mind is restored.

Hakuin also recommended using "sickness" itself as a *kōan*:
"First, use your illness to face death directly and solve that fun-

damental problem; second, rely on breath power to sustain
your life; third, reflect on how you will behave if you recover
and get a new lease on life."

In addition to such mental health techniques, Hakuin
devised a practical system of self-massage to keep the body fit:

(1) Massage the palm of each hand using the
thumb.

(2) Put the fingers of both hands together and
stretch them.

(3) Rub the hands together.

(4) Massage each thumb.

(5) Massage the tendons of each finger.

(6) Pull the fingers.

(7) Stretch out your arms and raise them.

(8) Massage the cheeks.

(9) Massage the nose on the left side and the
right.

(10) Massage the forehead from side to side.

(11) Massage under the eyebrows.

(12) Massage the ears in a downward direction.

(13) Pull the ears gently.

(14) Place the appropriate index finger in the ear
and lightly tap once.

(15) Massage the temples.

(16) Hold the head with both hands and tilt it all
the way back.

(17) Turn the head left and right.

(18) Twist the body first to one side, then the
other, three times.

(19) Perform nine full prostrations.

(20) Hold the hands together and raise them
above your head, then lower them.

(21) Rotate the shoulders.

(22) Pound the knees lightly with your fists.

(23) Pound the torso lightly with your fists.

Despite such solicitous concern for the physical and mental health of his disciples, a number of monks died during their training at Shōin-ji—nearly seventy tombstones are lined up behind Hakuin's grave.

By Ikkyū's time, calligraphy and painting had become a primary teaching vehicle of Zen. It was Hakuin, though, who brought the use of Zen art as "brushstrokes of enlightenment" to full flower. As already mentioned, after viewing a piece of Zen calligraphy, the young Hakuin burned his brushes in frustration: "the only way to create such profound brushwork is to perfect the mind." It was not until he was almost sixty, when he had mastered meditation in action, that Hakuin began painting seriously again.

Although obviously talented since birth, it is not clear where Hakuin acquired such technical skill with the brush. It is likely that he studied informally with Suiō, who was an excellent painter, and probably picked up some instruction from his sometime disciple Ike no Taiga, one of the great artists of the day. In the last three decades of his life, Hakuin produced a vast number of paintings on an extraordinary variety of subjects, ranging from full-color scenes, with a large number of characters and various themes and subthemes, to roughly drawn cartoons. Along with traditional Zen themes brushed in a strikingly fresh, highly personalized manner, Hakuin drew inspiration from other schools of Buddhism, Confucianism, Shintoism, Taoism, folk religion, and from everyday life (he often included his own and his parishioners' faces in paintings). His calligraphy, too, encompassed far more than the somber words of the Buddhas and Patriarchs, embracing nursery rhymes, popular ballads, humorous verse, and bawdy songs from the geisha quarters. Hakuin's works of art were "paintings that liberate beings," as one of his seals reads. They were visual sermons that made a far greater impact than a long, involved lecture or a commentary on a difficult text. Every one of Hakuin's students and parishioners could relate directly to the master's artistry, which had an immediate and lasting effect on the viewer.

In a sense, Hakuin's work was "anti-art," just as Zen is "anti-words." It was never consciously created to be beautiful or decorative. In fact, Hakuin never corrected mistakes or omissions in his calligraphy, and if the paper had drops on it or a cat's tracks, so much the better! On large pieces, Hakuin frequently did an outline first, but instead of erasing this, he drew over it, creating a kind of three-dimensional effect.

Hakuin's calligraphy was judged to be a powerful talisman, and his brushwork was widely sought. He wrote, "Rather than hanging fancy pictures in your homes, display paintings of Zen teachings in your alcove; honor that tradition with respect and you will be free from distress." To this day many antique dealers in Kyoto have at least one Hakuin piece in the shop to protect it against fire. Hakuin traveled a great deal in his sixties and seventies, and when he visited a private home he would often leave behind a piece or two of Zen art as payment. If the lodging was a lord's mansion, Hakuin might call for brush and ink and decorate a folding screen or paper sliding door on the spot.

Hakuin liked to caricature dilettante monks in his Zen art. He frequently lampooned Yoshida Kenkō (1283–1350), man of letters and author of *Essays in Idleness (Tsurezure-gusa)*, depicting him as a monkey foolishly trying to grasp the moon's reflection on water or writing the opening lines of that book on a piece of paper. Yoshida's Zen, the painting implied, was sham. Real Zen masters do not live in refined retirement, leisurely dabbling in art and religion. They are in the real world, constantly testing the quality of their enlightenment. That is why Hakuin did paintings representing Hotei, the "laughing Buddha," as a shopkeeper with this inscription: "Shopkeepers, too, must hear the sound of one hand clapping, otherwise business will stink!"

For prominent display in their alcoves, rich people might have a huge calligraphy of the character for "Virtue" inscribed with this bit of wisdom:

If you pile up money for your heirs, they will

surely waste it; if you collect books for them, they will likely not read a word. It is better to pile up virtue unobtrusively—such a legacy will last a long, long time.

Tight-fisted merchants who drove their employees too hard would receive this visual sermon from Hakuin:

> "*SYMPATHY*"
> They're your children, too,
> The people in your employ;
> Think of them
> As you would
> Your own beloved children.

Struggling disciples would get this heartening piece of calligraphy:

> "*PERSEVERANCE*"
> A quality greater
> Than any precept
> Or virtue:
> Perseverance makes
> People great.

Hakuin frequently brushed the character for "death" and added to it such inscriptions as:

> Young people!
> If you do not want to die,
> Then die now; if you die once,
> You won't die again!

> Anyone who sees
> Through death
> Becomes an ageless,
> Deathless Immortal.

Death, the great activator
Of the Patriarchs of old
And the basis of human life.

On occasion Hakuin would brush out a *kōan* such as "What is the nature of look, hear, learn, and know?" and instruct a trainee to hang it in his or her room and contemplate it morning and evening until the meaning became clear. Another favorite visual *kōan* was Yen-t'ou's "If you are the least bit inattentive, you are just like a corpse," that is, if your heart is not totally in what you are engaged in, your actions are dead.

Giant Half-Body Darumas—some over six feet tall—were Hakuin's trademark. His Darumas—actually self-portraits—are often inscribed with the battle cry of Hakuin-style Zen: "See into your nature and become the Buddha!" Other favored inscriptions were: "I've got my eye fixed on you [so hurry and wake up]!" and "Whichever way you look [you cannot escape my gaze, so get going]!" Hakuin was also capable of creating gentle images of Kannon, proving that he identified with the feminine principle as well as the masculine.

Hakuin admired Ikkyū (he even did a painting of Ikkyū carrying the skull around the streets of Kyoto on New Year's Day), but his own lifestyle was far more sober, and it appears that he was never sexually or emotionally involved with women (or men) during his long career as a Zen master. However, he clearly taught that sex, if properly utilized, was a valid form of meditation in action. He assigned the difficult "The monk and the young girl" *kōan* to all of his disciples, and brushed a large number of sex-charm paintings for his lay parishioners. Some were huge calligraphies of the single stroke representing the character *ichi*, "one," in the shape of gigantic phalluses with inscriptions such as "All things return to the *one*; where does the *one* return?" or "Even in the fiercest wind this doesn't waver!" Hakuin's favorite sex charm was a painting of a *bonseki*, a miniature landscape, that was in fact a disguised phallus, fully erect. On paintings of Mount Fuji—a conventional symbol of sexual union—Hakuin wrote this little

Giant Daruma (Bodhidharma), by Hakuin. (Murray Smith Collection, U.S.A.)
The inscription reads: "[Zen] points directly to the human heart; see into your nature and become the Buddha."

衆生福寿海

Kannon, the Goddess of Compassion, by Hakuin. (Genshin Collection, U.S.A.)

In addition to his fierce, masculine Darumas, Hakuin was capable of identifying with feminine expressions of love and compassion, and of reproducing these qualities in his masterful Zen art. The inscrip-tion reads: "An ocean of good fortune and longevity for sentient beings."

Hakuin's Motto: "Meditation in the MIDST of activity is a billion times superior to meditation in stillness!" (Tanaka Collection, Japan)

love song: "O lovely Miss Fuji, please shed your veil of clouds and show me your snow-white skin." And the heroine of many a Hakuin painting was Otafuku, the homely backwoods prostitute with a heart of gold who represented the unsullied love and pure compassion of Kannon.

Hakuin lived in semiretirement the last three years of his life, and the pieces produced in this period are extraordinarily lucid, clear, and powerful—bold manifestations of the profound insight of a true Zen master. There is today an increasing awareness in the East and the West that Hakuin's painting and calligraphy are as important to world cultural history as the art of Rembrandt. Dozens of first-rate Hakuin pieces are now in American and European collections, and exhibitions of his masterpieces have moved, inspired, and instructed people all over the world. (Incidentally, Hakuin was also an accomplished sculptor and carved many fine pieces, including, it is said, the glaring image of himself that sits in the hall of Shōin-ji.)

In his last year of life, the old master traveled to a temple to give a lecture. Upon his arrival, he suddenly collapsed, racked by violent chills. A middle-aged woman asked what she could do for him, and Hakuin replied, "Warm me with your body." Shedding her clothes, she embraced Hakuin, who then fell asleep for several hours in her arms, sweated out his sickness, and recovered.

The end was near, however, and in the winter of 1768, a doctor examined the failing master. As he felt Hakuin's pulse, the doctor told his patient, "Everything seems all right." "Some doctor," Hakuin grumbled. "He can't see that in three days I'll be gone." Hakuin's final piece of calligraphy was his life statement: a giant character for "midst" (*chū*), with the inscription, "Meditation in the MIDST of action is a billion times superior to meditation in stillness." At dawn of the eleventh day of the twelfth month, Hakuin awoke from a peaceful sleep, let loose a terrific shout, rolled over on his right side, and died.

After his cremation, Hakuin's ashes—divided among Shōin-ji, Ryūtaku-ji, and Muryō-ji—were said to be the lustrous color of coral and as fragrant as spice.

RYŌKAN TAIGU
(1758–1831)

RYŌKAN was born sometime in 1758 (the exact date is unknown) in the remote seaside village of Izumozaki in Echigo Province, now called Niigata Prefecture. This area of northern Honshū is "snow country," where in deep winter snowdrifts force residents to exit and enter their homes from the second floor. The district is also notorious for some of the worst earthquakes in Japan's history, and is famed for the lovely island of Sadō, place of exile for rebels and source of the shogun's gold, which was taken from its productive mines. Ryōkan's father, Inan (1738–95), was the hereditary village headman and Shintō priest. Inan was also a poet of some note, distantly associated with the Bashō school of haiku. Here is one of his verses:

> Ever changing,
> Summer clouds rise lazily,
> High above the hills.

Little is known of Ryōkan's mother other than that she was born on Sadō, but from what we can gather in Ryōkan's poems she seems to have been a gentle and loving person:

> In my dreams

Mother's form appears
Morning and night,
In the distant mist surrounding
The shores of Sadō.

Ryōkan's childhood name was Eizō. A quiet, studious boy who loved books, he was enrolled in a Confucian academy at around ten years of age and there received his basic education in the classics of China and Japan. Years later Ryōkan visited the grave of his first teacher, Ōmori Shiyō (d. 1791), and composed this touching poem in his memory:

An old grave hidden away at the foot of
  a deserted hill,
Overrun with rank weeds growing unchecked
  year after year;
There is no one left to tend the tomb,
And only an occasional woodcutter passes by.
Once I was his pupil, a youth with shaggy hair,
Learning deeply from him by the Narrow River.
One morning, I set off on my solitary journey
And the years passed between us in silence.
Now I have returned to find him at rest here.
How can I honor his departed spirit?
I pour a dipper of pure water over his tombstone
And offer a silent prayer.
The sun suddenly disappears behind the hill,
And I'm enveloped by the roar of the wind in
  the pines.
I try to pull myself away but cannot;
A flood of tears soaks my sleeves.

Under Shiyō's guidance Ryōkan developed a lifelong love of the classics of Confucius. Often his mother would send the boy out of the house to attend some village festivities, only to discover him later ensconced under a stone lantern in the garden reading the *Analects*. (When Ryōkan grew older he described the Chinese master not as a paragon of orthodoxy and stuffy correctness but as a warm, humble, and independent seeker after truth who was unjustly condemned by his contemporaries for impractical daydreaming!) As a youth, Ryōkan most of all enjoyed solitary walks along the shore facing the rough and stormy Sea of Japan or quiet reveries beneath an old pine tree in the family garden. Even as a child, he never told lies or argued with other boys.

The erratic and volatile Inan was eager to turn over the position of village headman to his eldest son as soon as Ryōkan came of age. Unfortunately—albeit for different reasons—the seventeen-year-old Ryōkan was ill-suited for the job. Honest and conciliatory by nature, he hated contention of any kind; totally guileless, he could not understand why others were not equally forthcoming. After undergoing a spiritual crisis, he decided to leave home and become a Buddhist monk.

A number of different explanations are given for this dramatic act: Ryōkan realized that he lacked the cunning required of a political leader; he was horrified by the bloody execution of a villager convicted of a serious crime (the headman had to serve as an official witness at such executions); he suddenly saw the light after a bout of dissolute living.

As a young man, the bookish Ryōkan apparently turned briefly into a Don Juan—"When that fellow is around," the villagers said of him, "better warn your daughters." According to one tale, Ryōkan was once at a party with his favorite geisha. The celebration continued far into the night, but he became increasingly morose. His lover did her best to cheer him up, but nothing could dispel his pervasive gloom. After spending all his money, he returned home in deep despair.

The following morning, his family found him with his head shaved and clad in a white kimono. Saying little, he departed for a nearby temple to seek admission as a novice. Along the way he happened to meet the geisha, who pleaded with him to reconsider. Ryōkan remained silent and continued resolutely on his way.

In truth, it was likely a combination of all these factors that led Ryōkan to renounce the world. Also, given his cultured upbringing—several other members of his family also joined the Buddhist priesthood—it is not surprising that he sought solace in religion. The position of headman went to Ryōkan's brother Yoshiyuki (1762–1834), who proved to be the worst administrator possible and eventually frittered away the family fortunes.

Ryōkan trained as a novice at Kōshō-ji, the local Sōtō Zen temple, for several years. Around 1780, the Zen master Kokusen (d. 1791) visited Kōshō-ji, and Ryōkan, who was deeply impressed by the sincere and earnest demeanor of the teacher, requested and received permission to formally become Kokusen's disciple. Consequently, they returned together to Entsū-ji, Kokusen's monastery in Tamashima (in present-day Okayama Prefecture).

Entsū-ji is a lovely little complex, containing a beautiful bamboo grove and lotus pond, that lies on a hill overlooking the harbor of Tamashima. (Most of the buildings from Ryōkan's time still stand.) Tamashima was a prosperous trading center, and Entsū-ji flourished under Kokusen's direction, there being never less than forty monks in training. Just like Ikkyū's teacher Kasō and Hakuin's teacher Shōju, Kokusen was a down-to-earth, no-nonsense master who declared his style of Zen to consist of "piling up stones, and hauling dirt." That is, the practice of Zen must be conducted in the midst of life's daily chores.

One of Ryōkan's favorite characters in the community was Senkei (n.d.), a monk who embodied Kokusen's teaching.

> Priest Senkei, a true man of the Way!
> He worked in silence—no extra words for him.
> For thirty years he stayed in Kokusen's
>   community.
> He never did meditation, never read the sutras,
> Never said a word about Buddhism—
> Just worked for the good of all.
> I saw him but did not really see him;

I met him but did not really meet him.
Ah, he is impossible to imitate,
Priest Senkei, a true man of the Way!

Ryōkan spent the next ten years at Entsū-ji devoting himself to Zen training and further study of the Chinese classics,
Buddhist sutras, poetry, and calligraphy. Late in life, Ryōkan
recalled his years at Entsū-ji in these poems:

At Entsū-ji so long ago—
How many times has winter given way to spring?
Beyond the gate a thousand homes,
Yet not a single acquaintance.
When my robe was soiled, I washed it;
If food ran out, we begged in the town.
I pored over the lives of eminent priests
And came to understand their praise of holy
    poverty.

Thinking back, I recall my days at Entsū-ji
And the solitary struggle to find the Way.
Carrying firewood reminded me of Layman Hō;
When I polished rice, the Sixth Patriarch came
    to mind.
I was always first in line to receive the Master's
    teaching,
And never missed an hour of meditation.
Thirty years have flown by
Since I left the green hills and blue sea of that
    lovely place.
What has become of all my fellow disciples?
And how can I forget the kindness of my
    beloved teacher?
The tears flow on and on, blending with the
    swirling mountain stream.

There were also some lighter moments at Entsū-ji for Ryōkan:

The long summer days at Entsū-ji!
Everything was fresh and pure.
Worldly sentiments never surfaced there.
In the cool shade reading poetry, beauty all
    around,
I endured the heat by listening
To the refreshing sound of the water wheel.

On the hill behind Entsū-ji we hid out in the
    woods,
Escaping from the heat and drinking saké to
    relax.
We emptied the flask and composed a few
    poems.
Not missed by the others we sat happily until the
    bell summoned us inside!

During his stay at Entsū-ji Ryōkan became enamored of
the writings of Dōgen (1200–53), the founder of the Sōtō Zen
School in Japan. He was especially fond of Dōgen's Four
Great Virtues: Charity, Kind Words, Good Works, and Empa-
thy. Ryōkan applied these virtues in concrete fashion, as we see
in this example. In those days, thieves often masqueraded as
monks, and ragamuffin Ryōkan was taken into custody several
times by the suspicious authorities when he was on his begging
rounds. Reminiscent of Hakuin and the baby incident, Ryōkan
similarly said nothing in his defense even when threatened with
a beating. His kind words, calm bearing, and non-violence prevailed, and he was released unharmed each time.

In 1790, at the age of thirty-two, Ryōkan was appointed
head monk at the monastery and presented with an *inka*.
Unlike the intense, almost melodramatic, enlightenment experiences of Ikkyū and Hakuin, Ryōkan apparently did not have
any single particularly overwhelming breakthrough; rather his
enlightenment was simply a natural flowering in line with the
low-key Sōtō Zen tradition of "just sitting like the Buddha" and
"practice and enlightenment are one."

When first ordained, he was called "Ryōkan Taigu." "*Ryō*" means "good," and "*kan* "signifies "broad" in the sense of generous and large-hearted. "*Taigu*" is "Great Fool," implying a childlike simplicity and a lack of pretense and sham. Kokusen referred to these qualities in the *inka* that he gave to his top disciple.

> Ryō appears foolish, but he traverses the broad
>   Way;
> Untrammeled, who can fathom him?
> I present this certificate along with a staff of
>   mountain wood;
> Wherever he wanders he will retain the peace
>   attained within these walls.

This document was Ryōkan's most treasured possession, and he kept it with him for the rest of his life.

Kokusen died the following year, and Ryōkan left Entsū-ji to embark on a long pilgrimage, drifting with the clouds and flowing with the water. Ryōkan seems to have stayed mostly in rural areas during this five-year period, sleeping in the fields or putting up briefly in makeshift huts and avoiding metropolitan centers and large monasteries. He did, however, seek out Zen Master Shūryū (n.d.) of Daitoku-ji, home temple of Ikkyū.

When Ryōkan reached the gates of Daitoku-ji, he was turned away coldly, being told that Shūryū was now living in retirement and not seeing anyone. Undeterred, Ryōkan sneaked into the temple grounds, jumped the massive wall, and waited outside the abbot's hermitage. Ryōkan then left a note addressed to Shūryū held down with a rock by the stone wash basin, hoping that the abbot would notice it when he emerged for the early morning service. Ryōkan was discovered by some monks, but as they were driving him away Shūryū appeared, read Ryōkan's sincere entreaty, and told him to visit any time he liked. Ryōkan later told his friends that he profited greatly from Shūryū's Rinzai-style teaching.

The only other account we have of Ryōkan's wanderings is

that of Kondō Manjō (d. 1848), who met him in southern Shikoku.

> When I was in my early twenties I traveled to the Tosa district. At dusk one day I was caught in a rainstorm, and since I was quite far from the castle town I sought shelter in a lonely little hut by the road. A shabbily dressed monk was living there who invited me in, with apologies that there was nothing to eat, nor was there any bedding. After our initial conversation, he said nothing but just sat silently in the meditation posture. I thought that he might be a bit weak in the head.
>
> I fell asleep, and the following morning he shared his thin gruel with me. The only things in the hut were a tiny Buddha image, a little desk, and two books. The one I picked up was a T'ang edition of the writings of Chuang-tzu; inside were copies of poems written by the hermit in beautiful cursive script. I then realized that this was no ordinary monk. I asked him to inscribe two blank fans that I had with me. On one he brushed a painting of plum blossoms and on the other Mount Fuji. He signed them "Ryōkan, native of Echigo." The monk refused to take any money but gladly accepted some calligraphy paper.

Ryōkan's mother had passed away during his stay at Entsū-ji, and his father, ever restless and temperamental, left home and ended up in Kyoto, where one of Ryōkan's brothers had achieved fame as a scholar. There, in 1795, the despondent Inan ended his troubled life by throwing himself in the Katsura River. Greatly saddened by the news of his father's tragic death, Ryōkan went to Kyoto to hold a memorial service for him, and then made a pilgrimage to the holy mountain of Kōya to pray for the repose of the souls of both his parents.

In Kyoto, Ryōkan received copies of his father's final poems and then wrote:

My father's
Poem cards become
Blurred with my tears
As I recall
Times together long ago.

As the Dharma-heir of Kokusen, one of the most highly regarded Sōtō Zen masters of the day, Ryōkan could have easily assumed the abbacy of a major temple, but the years of devoted poverty and freedom in the fields made him loath to be constrained by the burdens of a temple. Moreover, at that time there was fierce rivalry between the Eihei-ji and Sōji-ji factions of Sōtō Zen, and as an abbot Ryōkan would inevitably have been drawn into the conflict.

With no particular plan in mind, the forty-year-old Ryōkan drifted back to his native place, savoring the beauty spots and sacred sites of Japan along the way. When Ryōkan finally returned to Echigo, he recorded his thoughts in these two poems:

I have returned to my former village, and
Falling ill, I rest at a local inn.
I listen to the sound of the rain—
One robe, one bowl are all I have.
Becoming a little stronger, I lift my weak body,
Burn incense, and sit in meditation;
All night, rain falls sadly
As I dream of my long pilgrimage of past years.

Long ago I renounced the world to seek a true
    master,
Returning to my native village after twenty
    years,
My only possessions one robe, one bowl.

A statue of Ryōkan.
This stands near his grave on the grounds of the Kimura family
residence in Niigata Prefecture.

I ask after my old friends—
Most have become names on moss-covered
    tombstones.

One day, a weather-beaten monk turned up in Gomoto, a village about ten miles north of Izumozaki. He was given permission to take up residence in a run-down hut and soon became a common sight about the town. When he received more food than he needed for one day, he gave it to the birds and animals. The local people quickly recognized his virtue and began helping him with clothing as well as food, but the monk continued to pass along his possessions to beggars worse off than himself. Several of the villagers thought that the unusual monk looked vaguely familiar, so one of them paid him a visit. The hut was empty save for some beautifully written poems decorating the walls. The visitor made the connection and informed Ryōkan's family that their long-lost brother was home. Ryōkan, however, refused to return to his ancestral home and sent back most of the supplies his family sent.

Ryōkan lived in several hermitages in the neighborhood before finally settling down at Gogō-an, a sturdy structure isolated in a thick forest of ancient pines and cedars behind Kokujō-ji on Mount Kūgami. The name of the hermitage means "five cups," the stipend of rice received each day by the former Shingon abbot of Kokujō-ji, who had Gogō-an built for his retirement.

Ryōkan lived at Gogō-an from 1797 to 1802 and from 1804 to 1816. (Between 1802 and 1804, a retired abbot of Kokujō-ji used the hermitage, and during this period Ryōkan stayed at other Shingon temples in the area.) Ryōkan chose to be a hermit, but not the kind that shuts himself up in total isolation from humanity. Ryōkan hoped to emulate the Buddha, who was able to pass with equanimity between the realms of the sacred and the profane:

This is the Way He traveled to flee the world;
This is the Way He traveled to return to the world.

I, too, come and go along this Sacred Path
That bridges life and death, and traverses illusion.

As a hermit, Ryōkan perched himself on a meditation cushion and lived much like the Zen patriarchs of long ago, seeking
enlightenment deep in the mountains:

In the stillness by the empty window
I sit in formal meditation wearing my monk's
   surplice,
Navel and nose in alignment,
Ears parallel with shoulders.
Moonlight floods the room;
The rain stops, but the eaves drip and drip.
Perfect this moment—
In the vast emptiness, my understanding deepens.

At night, deep in the mountains,
I sit in meditation
The affairs of men never reach here;
Everything is quiet and empty,
All the incense has been swallowed up
   by the endless night.
My robe has become a garment of dew.
Unable to sleep I walk out into the woods—
Suddenly, above the highest peak,
   the full moon appears.

My life is poor
But my mind so clear
As I pass
Day after day
In this grass hut.

Like the little stream
Making its way
Through the mossy crevices,

I, too, quietly
Turn clear and transparent.

When all thoughts
Are exhausted
I slip into the woods
And gather
A pile of shepherd's purse.

Torn and tattered, torn and tattered,
Torn and tattered is this life.
Food? Wild vegetables from the roadside.
The shrubs and bushes advance toward my hut.
Often the moon and I sit together all night,
And more than once I have lost myself among
    the wild flowers,
Forgetting to return home.
No wonder I left the community life:
How could such a crazy monk live in a temple?

Living deep in the mountains, all of nature became Ryōkan's companion:

If your hermitage
Is deep in the mountains
Surely the moon,
Flowers, and crimson leaves
Will become your friends.

Wild peonies
Now at their peak
In glorious full bloom:
Too precious to pick,
Too precious not to pick.

"*Orchid*"
Deep in the valley, a beauty hides:

Serene, peerless, incomparably sweet.
In the still shade of the bamboo thicket
It seems to sigh softly for a lover.

The plants and flowers
I raised about my hut
I now surrender
To the will
Of the wind.

One spring day, Ryōkan noticed three bamboo shoots growing under his veranda. Bamboo grows rapidly, and soon the shoots were pushing against the bottom of of the floor. Ryōkan was anxious, for he did not like to see anything suffer, even plants. He decided to chop an opening in the floor and to burn a hole in the section of the thatched roof covering the veranda to permit the bamboo to grow unimpeded, but when Ryōkan put a candle to that part of the roof, the entire veranda caught fire and burned down. Ryōkan held a funeral service for the roasted bamboo, and then built a roofless veranda with sliding floorboards that would allow the bamboo shoots to slip through.

Although Ryōkan shunned the world, he did not loathe it:

It is not that
I do not wish
To mix with others
But living alone in freedom
Is a better Path for me.

When I think
About the misery
Of those in this world,
Their sadness
Becomes mine.

Oh, that my monk's robe

Was wide enough
To gather up all
The suffering people
In this floating world.

According to the "Ten Ox-herding Pictures," the culmina-
tion of Zen practice is to "return to the marketplace with bliss-
bestowing hands," and Ryōkan, like Ikkyū and Hakuin before
him, mingled with all manner of human beings—lords, beggars, farmers, merchants, fishmongers, innkeepers, courtesans,
children, outcasts—without condescension or revulsion.

Ryōkan was one of the few Japanese Buddhist monks who
lived entirely on alms. While Ikkyū and Hakuin spent some
time as mendicants, for the most part of their careers they—
like nearly every Buddhist cleric, past and present—relied on
either wealthy patrons or a regular group of parishioners for
support. Ryōkan, however, praised begging for food as the
"lifeblood of monastic life," a sacred practice established by
the Buddha himself, and he faithfully followed the rule of
poverty throughout his life.

The clouds are gone,
The sky is clear—
To beg for food
With a pure heart
Is a blessing from heaven.

"Food," Ryōkan once wrote, "should be received as bees
collect nectar from flowers; one should beg as unobtrusively as
moonlight illuminating a field." In one of his poems Ryōkan
stated: "I will call on every house, even those of wine merchants and fishmongers, just like the Prince of Beggars [the
Buddha]." Ryōkan also quoted from a sutra in which a Buddhist monk is reprimanded for singling out certain families to
beg from: "On your rounds all must be treated equally." Thus,
Ryōkan would stop, without hesitation, to beg in front of the
village brothel. In fact, if the girls were not busy they would

come out and play marbles with Ryōkan. When Yoshiyuki heard of his brother's amusing behavior, he teased Ryōkan with this poem:

> The black-robed monk
> Sports with
> Pleasure girls—
> What can be
> In his heart?

Ryōkan replied with this verse:

> Sporting and sporting,
> As I pass through this floating world.
> Finding myself here,
> Is it not good
> To dispel the bad dreams of others?

Yoshiyuki was still not satisfied:

> Sporting and sporting
> While passing through this world
> Is good, perhaps,
> But don't you think of
> The world to come?

Ryōkan's conclusion was:

> It is in this world,
> With this body
> That I sport.
> No need to think
> About the world to come.

Once Ryōkan was traveling with a young monk. At a certain teahouse they received food that contained fish. The young monk left the fish untouched, as is the orthodox Buddhist custom, but Ryōkan gobbled it down without a moment's thought.

"That food has fish in it, you know," the monk said to Ryōkan.

"Yes, it was delicious," Ryōkan said with a smile.

That evening they were put up by a farmer, and the following morning the young monk complained, "The fleas were biting like crazy, and I was up all night. But you slept like a baby. Why?"

"I eat fish when it is offered, but I also let the fleas and mosquitoes feast on me. Neither bothers me at all," Ryōkan replied matter-of-factly. (Ryōkan slept inside a mosquito net, not to protect himself but to protect the bugs—he feared he might accidentally kill them in his sleep. However, he left one leg outside the net so the insects would not go hungry.)

Like the Buddha, Ryōkan gratefully received whatever was put into his begging bowl:

> For our sakes
> The clams and fish
> Give themselves
> Unselfishly
> As food.

Ryōkan composed these poems about the nobility of begging:

> Spring—slowly the peaceful sound of
> The bell on my mendicant's staff drifts toward
>   the village.
> In the gardens, green willows;
> Waterplants float serenely on the pond.
> My bowl is fragrant from the rice of a thousand
>   homes;
> My heart has renounced the sovereignty of riches
>   and fame.
> Quietly cherishing the memory of the ancient
>   Buddhas,
> I walk to the village for another day of begging.

After spending the day begging in the village
I sit peacefully under a cliff in the evening cool.
Alone, with one robe, one bowl—
The life of a Zen monk is truly the most free!

According to orthodox Buddhism, it is the almsgiver who should be grateful since he or she is acquiring merit by donating food to a monk, but Ryōkan was ever mindful of one of the verses used in the Zen Buddhist grace: "Recall the great effort of farmers to grow this food." Rather than staring straight ahead in silence and receiving the food without acknowledgment, as custom dictated, Ryōkan would hold up his bowl reverently with a heart full of gratitude each time he was given alms. Ryōkan would bow deeply and ask for the Buddha's blessing whenever he passed farmers laboring away in the rice paddies, and he spent many hours in his hermitage chanting sutras on their behalf.

Spring rains,
Summer showers,
A dry autumn.
May nature smile on us
And we all will share in the bounty.

If the harvest was especially good, Ryōkan would occasionally help himself. Once he left this poem on a tree in the grove of a local farmer.

Please don't mistake me
For a bird
When I swoop
Into your garden
To eat the crab apples.

Sometimes the alms were unexpected:

After gathering firewood in the mountains

I returned to my hut
And found pickled plums and potatoes
Left beneath my window by a visitor.
The plums were wrapped in paper,
The potatoes in green grass,
And a scrap of paper bore the donor's name.
Deep in the mountains the food is tasteless—
Mostly turnips and greens—
So I quickly boiled the treat with soya paste and
    salt.
I filled my usually empty stomach
With three big bowls.
If my friend had left some saké
It would have been a real banquet.
I savored about a fifth of the gift and stored the
    rest;
Patting my full belly, I went back to my chores.
Buddha's Enlightenment Day will be here in six
    days
And I did not know what to offer,
But now I have become rich—
Buddha will feast on plums and delicious potato
    gruel.

Ryōkan was famed for not wasting a crumb of food. If anything was left over, he put it into a clay pot. Naturally, the accumulated food fermented and rotted, becoming full of maggots. A visitor once saw Ryōkan eat from the pot.

"Don't eat that," the visitor exclaimed, "it's spoiled and has grubworms in it."

"No, no, it's all right," Ryōkan reassured him. "I let the maggots escape before I eat it and it tastes just fine!"

Ryōkan regularly shared his food with the birds and stray dogs and cats. Along with the good times, though, there were also the bad:

In the blue sky a winter goose cries;

The mountains are bare, nothing but fallen
   leaves.
Twilight—returning along the chill path,
Alone, carrying an empty rice bowl.

No begging
Again today
In the village.
The snow falls
And falls.

No luck today on my mendicant rounds;
From village to village I dragged myself.
At sunset I find myself with miles of mountains
   between me and my hut.
The wind tears at my frail body
And my little bowl looks so forlorn—
Yet this is my chosen Path that guides me
Through disappointment and pain, cold and
   hunger.

Even though Ryōkan depended entirely on alms he would
often become intoxicated by the beauty of the seasons while on
his rounds.

I went there
To beg rice,
But the blooming bush clover
Among the stones
Made me forget the reason.

Ryōkan was very fond of his rough little begging bowl,
itself a donation from a family that once used it as a kitchen
pot.

In my little begging bowl
Violets and dandelions

Mixed together
As an offering to the
Buddhas of the Three Worlds.

Picking violets
By the roadside I absentmindedly
Left my little bowl behind—
O poor little bowl!

I've forgotten my
Little begging bowl again—
No one will take you,
Surely no one will take you,
My sad little bowl!

On his rounds Ryōkan would often stop to help families with kitchen work—cleaning vegetables, chopping wood, preparing the fire. If there was nothing specific to do, he sat quietly in a corner doing *zazen.* He was also an excellent folk healer and would treat sick family members with massage, moxibustion, and herbal medicines. However, when the family asked him to visit them again the next day, the monk invariably replied, "Sorry, no promises. We never know what the next day will bring."

Ryōkan liked to stop and play *kusa-awase* (tug-of-war using thick weeds bound together) with the village boys and *temari* (rhythmic catch using a cloth ball) with the village girls.

Once again the children and I are fighting a battle
　　using spring grasses.
Now advancing, now retreating, each time with
　　more refinement.
Twilight—everyone has returned home;
The bright, round moon helps me endure the
　　loneliness.

First days of spring, blue sky, bright sun.

Everything is gradually becoming fresh and
   green.
Carrying my bowl I walk slowly to the village.
The children, surprised to see me,
Joyfully crowd about, bringing
My begging trip to an end at the temple gate.
I place my bowl on top of a white rock and
Hang my sack from the branch of a tree.
Here we play with the wild grasses and throw
   a ball.
For a time I play catch while the children sing;
Then it is my turn.
Playing like this, here and there, I have forgotten
   the time.
Passersby point and laugh at me, asking,
"What is the reason for such foolishness?"
No answer I give, only a deep bow;
Even if I replied they would not understand.
Look around, there is nothing besides this!

Ryōkan was known as the "Master of *Temari*" in the province, and always kept two or three cloth balls in his sleeves,
ready to pull out as soon as any children appeared:

We throw a little cloth ball back and forth.
I don't want to boast of my skill but . . .
If someone asks the secret of my art, I tell him,
One, two, three, four, five, six, seven!

Playing *temari*
With the village children
This warm, misty
Spring day—
No one wants it to end.

In the ten quarters of the Buddha-land
There is only one Vehicle.

When we see clearly, there is no difference in all
  the teachings.
What is there to lose? What is there to gain?
If we gain something, it was there from the
  beginning;
If we lose anything, it is hidden nearby.
Look at the cloth ball in my sleeve—
Surely it is the precious jewel of enlightenment!

    Ryōkan loved children and wrote many poems about his lit-
tle friends.

Children!
Shall we go
To Iyahiko
To see the hill
Full of blooming violets?

Hand in hand
The children and I
Pick spring vegetables.
What could be
More wonderful?

The ninth month has just begun
As we walk to Pine Tail Ridge.
A solitary goose flies overhead,
The chrysanthemums are in full bloom.
The children and I have come to this pine wood.
We have only walked a short distance,
But the world is hundreds of miles away.

As I watch
The children happily playing,
Without realizing it
My eyes
Fill with tears.

Spring is here,
The trees are in full bloom,
And last autumn's leaves are gone.
I must hurry to
Meet the children!

Once Ryōkan was playing hide-and-seek with the children and he ran to hide in a nearby shed. The children knew where he was and decided to play a joke on him—they ran away without letting him know the game was over. The following morning a farmer's wife came into the shed and was startled to find Ryōkan crouching in the corner. "What are you doing here, Ryōkan?" she asked. "Shh, be quiet, please," he whispered, "or else the children will find me."

Ryōkan was expert at playing dead. He would keel over and let the children bury him with grass and leaves. Once the children noticed that he was not breathing. "Oh, no!" they wailed. "Ryōkan really is dead this time!" All of a sudden Ryōkan sprang up with a shout, scaring the children. Long years of meditation and breath control had trained Ryōkan to hold his breath and remain perfectly still for minutes at a time.

Another time Ryōkan was walking near the village when he heard a small voice cry, "Help! Help me, please!" A little boy was stuck in the topmost branches of a persimmon tree. Ryōkan helped the lad down and said that he would pick some fruit for him. Ryōkan climbed the tree and picked one of the persimmons. He decided to taste it first, since unripe persimmons can be quite astringent, and he did not want to disappoint the boy. Ryōkan found the persimmon very sweet, so he picked one more, and it, too, was sweet. One after another, he stuffed the succulent persimmons into his mouth, exclaiming, "Oh, how sweet!" He had completely forgotten about the little boy waiting hungrily below until the lad yelled, "Ryōkan! Please give me some persimmons!" Ryōkan came to senses, laughed, and passed the delicious fruit to his small friend.

Ryōkan wrote this memorial poem for all the children who died one year in a smallpox epidemic:

When spring comes
From the tip of every branch
Flowers will bloom,
But the crimson leaves of
Last year, the little ones,
Will never again return.

Ryōkan also enjoyed sipping saké—the "hot water of transcendental wisdom" and the "best of all medicines"—with the local farmers during lulls in their work:

Walking besides a clear running river,
    I come to a farmhouse.
The evening chill has given way to the warmth
    of the sun.
Sparrows gather in a bamboo grove,
    voices chirping here and there.
I meet the old farmer returning from the fields;
He greets me like a long-lost friend.
At his cottage, the farmer's wife heats saké
While we eat freshly picked vegetables and chat.
Together, gloriously drunk, we no longer know
The meaning of unhappiness.

Midsummer—
I walk about with my staff.
Old farmers spot me
And call me over for a drink.
We sit in the fields
Using leaves for plates.
Pleasantly drunk and so happy,
I drift off peacefully
Sprawled out on a paddy bank.

Drinking sweet saké
With the farmers
While our eyebrows

Turn white
With snow.

Tomorrow?
The day after?
Who knows?
We are drunk
On today!

Sometimes Ryōkan enjoyed dropping in on old friends. His companions said of him:

> When Ryōkan visits it is as if spring had come on a dark winter's day. His character is pure and he is free of duplicity and guile. Tall and thin, Ryōkan resembles one of the immortals of ancient literature and religion. There is not the slightest sanctimoniousness about him, and he radiates warmth and compassion. He never gets angry and will not listen to criticism of others. His voice is always clear and bright. When he stays at a home all family problems seem to dissipate and the house remains peaceful days after his visit. Mere contact with him brings out the best in people.

While other Buddhist priests lectured for hours on the profundity of the sutras or officiated at elaborate (and costly) ceremonies, Ryōkan simply wandered about in tattered robes, always smiling and bowing to all, a living sermon not unlike St. Francis of Assisi, "God's Fool." Ryōkan's patron saint was Jōfukyō, "Never-despising Bodhisattva."

In the morning, bowing to all;
In the evening, bowing to all.
Respecting others is my only duty—
Hail to Never-despising Bodhisattva.

In heaven and earth, he stands alone.

A real monk
Needs
Only one thing—
A heart like
Never-despising Bodhisattva.

Ryōkan gently chided fellow Buddhists for their preoccupation with details and categories, words and concepts:

When I see learned priests lecturing on the
   sutras,
Their eloquence seems to flow in circles;
The Five Periods of the Law and the Eight
   Doctrines—
Nice theories, but who needs them?
Pedants have swelled heads,
But ask them matters of real importance
And all you get is empty babble.
The Buddha proclaimed countless teachings,
Each one revealing the purest truth.
Just as each breeze and every drop of rain
Refreshes the forest.
There is no sutra that does not lead to salvation.
Grasp the essence of each branch,
And stop trying to rank the Buddha's teaching.

Nothing makes me
Happier
Than Amida's vow
To save
Everyone.

In one of the villages there was a ferryman who was a great
troublemaker. He was annoyed by everyone's constant praise
of Ryōkan, and when it happened that Ryōkan asked to be

taken across on this man's ferry, he violently rocked the boat, and Ryōkan was thrown into the river. Ryōkan almost drowned before the ferryman pulled him out. Unaware that the ferryman had deliberately caused him to fall overboard, Ryōkan thanked the man profusely. The ferryman was not expecting such a response and began to feel remorse for this and all his other bad actions. He brought Ryōkan to the bank and the monk again expressed his deep gratitude. Later on, when Ryōkan came back for the return trip, the ferryman confessed his evil deed and begged for Ryōkan's forgiveness. Ryōkan just smiled and told him not to worry about it. They shared a jug of saké together and the ferryman thereafter mended his ways.

Another time Ryōkan was attacked by a crazed Buddhist priest in a drunken rage. Ryōkan calmly took the priest's blows until he was subdued by the villagers. That night a storm broke, but Ryōkan, who was staying at a friend's home, suddenly went outside. The friend, concerned for Ryōkan's safety, followed him, to see Ryōkan cover the mad priest, who was sleeping off his drunken stupor in a field, with a straw raincoat.

Once a relative of Ryōkan's asked him to speak to his delinquent son. Ryōkan came to visit the family but did not say a word of admonition to the boy. He stayed overnight and prepared to leave the following morning. As the wayward boy was helping tie Ryōkan's straw sandals, he felt a drop of warm water on his shoulder. Glancing up, he saw Ryōkan looking down at him, his eyes full of tears. Ryōkan returned to Gogō-an, and the boy had a complete change of heart.

Ryōkan never sought disciples, but he did have one friend, Saichi, who was a kindred spirit. When Saichi died, Ryōkan grieved:

> Ah . . . my Zen layman.
> You studied with me two decades;
> You were the one who truly
> Understood the things
> The others missed completely.

The samurai lord of a local domain wanted to construct a magnificent temple and install Ryōkan as its head priest. He went to see Ryōkan at Gogō-an, but Ryōkan was out picking flowers and the lord and his party had to wait quite a while before he returned with his begging bowl full of fragrant blossoms. The lord made his request, but Ryōkan remained silent. Then he brushed this haiku and handed it to the lord:

> The wind brings
> Enough fallen leaves
> To make a fire.

The lord nodded in understanding and returned to his castle.

Once a misdirected thief entered Gogō-an but naturally found nothing of value. Out of frustration the thief took Ryōkan's old and torn sleeping quilt and his meditation cushion. When Ryōkan returned to the hut and discovered what had happened he wrote this haiku:

> The thief left it behind—
> The moon
> At the window.

Ryōkan loved to join in the all-night dances of the midsummer Bon Festival, but since he was a monk he had to disguise himself by wearing a big kerchief and a woman's kimono. All the villagers knew, of course, that it was Ryōkan, and one year several of the villagers decided to tease him. "Who is that charming girl?" they whispered among themselves just loud enough for Ryōkan to hear. "She certainly is a good dancer!" Extremely pleased, he lost himself in the role of a female dancer, swaying to and fro with feminine grace.

Ryōkan disliked pomp and ceremony. One day he was invited to a formal tea ceremony at a wealthy family's home. The host was proud of his elegant, expensive utensils, and the other guests were turned out in kimono of costly Kyoto brocade. When Ryōkan, attired as usual in his shabby, patched up robe, sipped the thick tea, he made a face and exclaimed, "How bitter—this tastes awful!" He then spat the tea back into the bowl. To further disrupt the proceedings, Ryōkan picked his nose and tried to deposit its contents on the sleeve of the haughty guest sitting next to him.

Even though Ryōkan was content with his life as a hermit, there were still periods of deep loneliness:

> Sometimes I sit quietly,
> Listening to the sound of falling leaves.
> Peaceful indeed is the life of a monk,
> Cut off from all worldly matters.
> Then why do I shed these tears?

> In this world
> If there were one
> Of like mind—
> We could spend the night
> Talking in my little hut!

Ryōkan was delighted to have visitors, and he often sent poetic invitations to his friends:

> If you are not put off
> By the voice of the valley
> And the starry peaks,
> Why not walk through the shady cedars
> And come see me?

> Spring has begun!
> Jewels and gold
> Everywhere—
> Please, please
> Pay me a visit.

> The branches that will
> Serve as autumn firewood

Are still in bloom—
Please gather grass kissed with dew
And come visit me.

At dusk
Come to my hut—
The crickets will
Serenade you, and I will
Introduce you to the moonlit woods.

When visitors called on Ryōkan, he would bring them a
bowl to use as a wash basin. They would protest, "That is your
food bowl—we can't use that to wash our hands in!"

"No, no," Ryōkan would assure them. "It is the only bowl I
have and it serves quite well for cooking, as a water bowl, and
as a wash basin. And what is even better, I found it abandoned
in a thicket. Someone had thrown it away, but I gave it a new
home!"

Bōsai (1752–1826), a famous scholar from the capital city
of Edo, long wanted to meet the eccentric Zen monk of Echigo.
He made his way to Ryōkan's hut, but when he reached it
Ryōkan was sitting in meditation on the veranda. Bōsai, not
wishing to disturb him, waited until Ryōkan finished, almost
three hours later. Ryōkan was overjoyed to meet the famous
scholar, and they talked of poetry, philosophy, and literature
for the rest of the day. As evening approached, Ryōkan wanted
to get some saké. Ryōkan asked Bōsai to wait a bit while he ran
down to a farmhouse to borrow some. Bōsai waited and waited
but Ryōkan did not return.

Finally, Bōsai went to look for him. To his astonishment,
he saw him about a hundred yards from the hermitage, sitting
under a pine, gazing dreamily at the full moon.

"Ryōkan! Where have you been? I've been waiting for you
for hours! I thought something had happened to you!"

"Bōsai-san! You have arrived just in time. Isn't the moon
splendid?"

"Yes, yes, it's wonderful. But where is the saké?"

"The saké? Oh, yes, the saké. Please forgive me. I'll get some right away!" Ryōkan sprang up and bounded down the path, leaving Bōsai standing in amazement.

When friends called, Ryōkan often greeted them with poems:

> Deep in the woods,
> Holed up for the winter
> An old fellow like me—
> Who will be the first to visit?
> I knew it would be you!

> During a lull in the rain
> I picked some
> Wild parsley
> For you to enjoy
> During your visit.

> How heartless
> For the snowflakes
> Not to fall
> On the day
> Of your esteemed visit.

To friends about to depart, Ryōkan wrote:

> Wait for moonlight
> Before you go—
> The mountain trail
> Is thick with
> Chestnut burrs!

> Dew-covered, the mountain
> Trail will be chill.
> Before you leave
> How about
> One last cup of warm saké?

In neither the marketplace nor his hermitage was Ryōkan a cold-hearted, misanthropic ascetic:

> All night long
> In my grass hut
> Warmed by brushwood
> We talked and talked.
> How can I forget that wonderful evening.

> Descending to the valley to gather orchids
> The ground was blanketed with frost and dew,
> And it took all day to find the flowers.
> Suddenly I thought of an old friend
> Separated from me by miles of mountains and
>   rivers.
> Will we ever meet again?
> I gaze toward the sky,
> Tears streaming down my cheeks.

As with Ikkyū and Hakuin, poetry and calligraphy were central to Ryōkan's Zen, and his verses served as unobtrusive Buddhist sermons. Technically, Ryōkan was influenced by the classics of Chinese and Japanese poetry, but he pretty much wrote as he pleased and in general ignored the rules of composition:

> Who says my poems are poems?
> My poems are not poems.
> After you know that my poems are not poems,
> Then we can begin to discuss poetry!

Ryōkan felt a special affinity with Han-shan (Kanzan), the legendary Chinese Zen eccentric and poet of the T'ang dynasty. (Han-shan was also a great favorite of Hakuin, who authored a lengthy commentary on Han-shan's poems and depicted him frequently in art.) Here is one typical verse of Han-shan's:

Calligraphy Practice Sheet. (Private collection, Japan)
Throughout his life, Ryōkan devoted himself to the study of calligraphy, and today even his practice sheets are valued as masterpieces.

My home is a cave, without a thing in it—
Pure and marvelously empty,
As bright and clear as the sun.
A dish of mountain vegetables is sufficient,
And a patched cloak is plenty of cover for me.
Let a thousand wizards show up to grant me any
    wish!
I already have the Supreme Buddha
    in my possession!

Ryōkan composed this poem in the same vein:

Returning home from a day of begging;
Sage has covered my door.
Now, a bunch of leaves burns with the brushwood.
Silently, I read the poems of Han-shan,
Accompanied by the autumn wind rustling
    through the reeds.
I stretch out both feet and lie down.
What is there is fret over?
What is there to doubt?

Ryōkan's calligraphy is even more highly esteemed than his poetry—the subtle beauty and the delightfully irregular shape of his characters combine with the purity and warmth manifest in each brushstroke for an effect perhaps unequaled in Japanese art. In fact, the popularity of Ryōkan's poetry and calligraphy with connoisseurs is ironic, for Ryōkan once said that among the few things he disliked were "poetry by a poet, and calligraphy by a calligrapher."

Ryōkan practiced calligraphy continually, reverently brushing the *Thousand Character Classic* each morning, and blackening his practice sheets. Even on his begging rounds he would use his finger to trace characters in the air or in the sand at his feet. Since his calligraphy was valued so highly, all kinds of people began pestering Ryōkan for a specimen of his brushwork:

I shaved my head, became a Zen monk,
And spent years making my Way through the
    tangled weeds.
But now, all people say to me is,
"Brush us some poetry! Brush us some poetry!"

When people began greedily requesting his calligraphy just to display it, while ignoring the Zen content, Ryōkan started putting them off with excuses. This lead to an amusing battle of wits.

Once a rich merchant who greatly desired some of Ryōkan's calligraphy told the guileless monk that a famous artist was to visit his home. He invited Ryōkan to meet the artist, and when Ryōkan arrived at the merchant's home, Ryōkan was led into a large room that had been especially prepared for the work of a master: fragrant, freshly ground ink, a set of the best brushes, piles of calligraphy paper. "The artist will be here soon," the merchant fibbed. "Please feel free to use these materials until he arrives." As the merchant had calculated, Ryōkan could not resist, and soon the room was full of Ryōkan's brushwork. When Ryōkan came out of his reverie, he thought that the merchant would be furious at him for using up all the ink and paper so he sheepishly slipped out of the house. The merchant had what he wanted. In a similar tale, Ryōkan was left alone in a room with freshly papered doors. He became carried away by the whiteness of the new paper and brushed poems of Han-shan all over it. Although it was unplanned, the master of the house was delighted and had the paper removed and mounted on a screen.

Ryōkan adored flowers, and one of his friends by the name of Yamada had a garden full of magnificent peonies. Yamada would not let anyone touch the precious flowers, but one day he caught Ryōkan, who could contain himself no longer, trying to sneak off with a branch. Seeing a chance to get some calligraphy from Ryōkan, Yamada shouted, "Even if you are a Zen master, you still can't get away with this!"

Yamada took the embarrassed Ryōkan to the village constable and had him shut up in a little room. Yamada made a sketch of Ryōkan making off with the peonies and said to the monk. "Listen here, Flower-Thief! I'll let you go if you brush an inscription on this sketch." Ryōkan wrote contritely:

Ryōkan caught
Red-handed
Stealing the flowers.
Now everyone
Will always know.

A masterpiece of Japanese calligraphy was also acquired by similarly devious means. When Ryōkan approached a group of children making kites, they cried, "Ryōkan! Ryōkan! Please write something that will help make our kites fly!" Ryōkan thought for a moment and then brushed on the paper they had brought him "Heaven–Up–Great–Wind." The beauty of those four characters—among the simplest in the Japanese language and known to every child—written spontaneously with a borrowed brush on paper placed on the ground, is indescribable, and the piece is a true treasure. But the children had been put up to asking for it by a clever neighbor!

In many cases, though, Ryōkan had the upper hand. Once he was tricked into going upstairs in a big building and was stranded there when the family took the ladder away. "We won't let you down until you do some calligraphy for us," they told the captive. "Very well," Ryōkan said. He dashed off some calligraphy, held the brushwork up for them to see, and they put the ladder back. The brushwork was difficult to read but later they found out that all the sheets said the same thing: "Without a ladder, I've got no feet."

In a similar situation, when Ryōkan was caught in a downpour and needed shelter he was obliged to write inscriptions on several fans. Each one read, "When it rains, Ryōkan is so sad." On another occasion, a fellow brought some paper to Ryōkan and told him, "People are saying your calligraphy is not as good as it used to be because you do not practice enough. Here, you can practice on this." Ryōkan scribbled over and over, "Sugar is sweet, medicine is bitter."

Ryōkan once did a painting of a skull, a favorite theme of Zen artists, for a priest friend. The priest wanted Ryōkan to add an inscription, but Ryōkan thought the painting was fine as it was. The priest persisted, though, asking Ryōkan to write something each time he visited. Finally, Ryōkan brushed this inscription: "Today, Ryōkan has written something."

Once, after the long winter confinement, Ryōkan's barber shaved half his shaggy head and then demanded "ransom" to shave the rest: a sample of Ryōkan's calligraphy. Ryōkan brushed the name of a Shintō god. This kind of calligraphy served as a good luck charm, so the barber had it mounted and hung the calligraphy in his alcove. One day a friend said, "There is a character missing from that god's name." Such an omission negates the effect of the calligraphy as a talisman, and when the barber confronted Ryōkan, he was told, "You short-changed me so I shortchanged you. That nice old lady down the road always gives me an extra bean-cake so the calligraphy I gave her has the other character in it!"

Ryōkan loved to play the board game *go*, but he hated to lose, though, which was unfortunate since he wasn't a strong player. After one close defeat he wanted a rematch, and his opponent agreed, "Only if you promise to give me a piece of calligraphy each time you lose." Ryōkan reluctantly agreed, but he lost again and again. His opponent expected several prize pieces of Zen wisdom, but all he got on each sheet was:

> Picking persimmons—
> My testicles are frozen
> By the autumn wind.

Ryōkan often left out characters accidentally when he brushed long poems or quotations from memory, and once someone complained about this. Ryōkan responded, "Anyone who can read my calligraphy can easily supply the missing character; those who can't read won't miss it!"

A friend of Ryōkan asked for a piece of calligraphy that would bring good luck and prosperity to his family. Ryōkan brushed the single syllable "*shi*" on a full-sized sheet of paper. "What does it mean?" the friend asked. Reminiscent of Haku-in's *kōan*, Ryōkan replied, "Death. When people are mindful of death, they don't waste time or squander their wealth!"

Once the owner of a soy sauce shop in Nagaoka made the long trip to Ryōkan's hut with a special request. The signboard in front of his shop was poorly written and the owner felt that this was keeping customers away. Would Ryōkan please help him by writing a new signboard? Ryōkan agreed and brushed "Vinegar–Soy sauce–Joshuya." The shopkeeper was extremely pleased and proudly displayed the board upon his return. A few days later, Bōsai (who was mentioned earlier) happened to pass by the store and saw the sign. Bōsai went in, informed the shopkeeper that the signboard was too precious to subject to the wind and rain, and brushed a new one. Bōsai's signboard was put out, but then it was spotted by another calligrapher of only slightly less renown than Ryōkan and Bōsai. This situation was repeated a fourth time—the store flourished and the shopkeeper became the proud possessor of four magnificent signboards.

Sometimes Ryōkan's fame as a calligrapher came in handy. On one journey, Ryōkan was obliged to hire a pack-horse to negotiate a dangerous mountain path. He didn't have any money to pay the sixteen *sen* fee so he told the driver, "You can hit me sixteen times on the head." The driver had recognized Ryōkan and said, "No. Write me sixteen characters on this paper and I'll waive the charge." Similarly, when Ryōkan met a traveler in need of lodging, all he had to do was write a little letter of introduction: "Show this to anyone in the village and you'll be sure to find lodgings."

In addition to the kite calligraphy mentioned previously, two other Ryōkan masterpieces are "One–Two–Three, *I–Ro–Ha* [A–B–C]" and "Heart–Moon–Circle." The first pair of hanging scrolls were brushed for a shopkeeper who asked for something simple that everyone could read. The second

The Buddha's Parinirvana, by Ryōkan. (Private collection, Japan)
A rare example of a Zen painting by Ryōkan. The brushwork is guileless and totally unaffected, and is infused with a gentle humor.

was done in the kitchen of one of Ryōkan's friends. The old wooden lid that covered the family rice pot had split and it was placed aside for firewood. Ryōkan felt sorry for the lid, so he brushed "Heart–Moon–Circle" across it, knowing that they wouldn't destroy the lid if it had his calligraphy on it. The brushwork was so sublime that the family had the lid repaired and the calligraphy engraved into the wood.

Among the most treasured possessions of the people in Ryōkan's neighborhood were the letters that they received from the eccentric monk during his years at Gogō-an and Otogo Shrine. As he grew increasingly infirm with age it became difficult for Ryōkan to go out on daily begging rounds, and his friends began providing his simple needs—a cotton robe, a pair of *tabi* socks, a cloth hat, incense, a *temari* ball, tea, rice, soya paste, tobacco, pickles, oil, *wasabi* (horseradish), fruit, vegetables, saké, and, as a treat, sweet cakes—by messenger. Whenever Ryōkan received such alms he sent a little note or poem acknowledging the gift and thanking the donor for his or her great generosity. In fact, the surest way to get a sample of Ryōkan's calligraphy was to give him a donation—he always sent a thank-you note! Here are two such poems:

> Dulse,
> Saké, and *wasabi*:
> With such fine gifts
> My spring is
> No longer lonely!

> "*A Gift of Seven Pomegranates*"
> Splitting them,
> Picking them apart,
> Breaking them in two:
> Eating, eating, eating—
> Not letting them out of my mouth!

If Ryōkan happened to run low on supplies he would send poems of request:

The weather is good and
I have many visitors
But little food.
Any pickled plums
To spare?

It has grown chill
And the firefly
Glows no longer:
Will some kind soul
Send me golden water?

("Firefly" was one of Ryōkan's nicknames; "golden water" is saké.) On the rare occasions Ryōkan was given money, he would carefully brush a receipt, a kind of calligraphic I.O.U. that was later mounted and displayed as a work of art. Once Ryōkan wrote a relative, "I have accumulated a large amount of money. Please come get it." The fortune turned out to be single silver coin.

Incidentally, someone told Ryōkan that if you find money on the road you will be very happy. One day, after he received several coins during a begging trip, he decided to see if that was true. Ryōkan scattered the coins along the road and then picked them up. He did this several times without experiencing any thrill and wondered what the person had meant. Ryōkan tried it a few more times and in the process he lost all the money in the grass. After searching for a long time he finally found the coins he had lost. Ryōkan was very happy. "Now I understand," he thought. "To find money is indeed a joy."

Ryōkan would also send letters of request to scholar friends for books and shared the fruits of his own studies. From the following letter it appears that Ryōkan was well acquainted with Hakuin's work *Evening Chat on a Boat*:

This winter I have been applying the teachings
of the Taoist sage Hakuyū and have learned this:
    I avoid chasing after this and that,

And keep my mouth closed in strict silence.
I take food only when my stomach is empty
And clack my teeth after waking from a dream.
I'm reading the story of Hakujū
And have learned about maintaining good
   health
By keeping my *ki* well balanced.
And not being disturbed by things wicked or
   base.

Ryōkan traded recipes for herbal medicine with scholar friends and also requested them to send him their spare ink, brushes, and paper.

Once Ryōkan sent this New Year's greeting to a monk friend:

> "*Greetings for the New Year!*"
> Tomorrow will mark the arrival of spring:
> There is no help for it!
> My heart beats
> Faster and faster
> And I cannot sleep:
> Spring comes tomorrow.

Following the terrible earthquake of 1831, in which 10,000 homes were destroyed and 1,200 people perished, Ryōkan sent this reflective letter to a concerned friend:

> The earthquake was dreadful. My little hut was spared. It is fortunate that there was no loss of life among your friends and family. When such disasters occur we must not succumb to despair; when death confronts us we must meet it head on. Even death and disaster have a place in the nature of things. Still . . .

> Face to face

With death,
Yet living on to
See the world suffer
Seems too sad to bear.

Ryōkan sent many letters to his wayward brother, Yoshi-yuki:

How are you doing
These days, my little brother?
The snow is thawing
But the wind still
Blows so cold.

Other letters thanked Yoshiyuki for gifts, particularly a piece of tanned leather that the frugal Ryōkan used as a cape, a coverlet, and a carpet. Ryōkan also gently pleaded with his brother to stop wasting himself on wine and women, reminding him in a letter that "contentment is the true wealth."

One day a messenger came to Ryōkan's hut with a letter that needed an immediate response. At that time Ryōkan was engrossed in trying to spin his begging bowl on top of a stick, a trick he had seen performed by traveling street entertainers. Ryōkan dashed off a reply, but soon the messenger was back.

"My master is angry with me. He can make no sense of your reply and thinks that I must have misunderstood your instructions."

When Ryōkan looked at his letter he saw that it said, "The bowl should spin and spin."

"Oh, I'm so sorry," Ryōkan apologized to the messenger. "This time I'll give you the correct answer!"

Since Ryōkan was so forgetful he wrote himself memos and lists of various things he should remember:

Take care not to:
talk too much;
talk too fast;

talk without being asked to;
talk gratuitously;
talk with your hands;
talk about worldly affairs;
talk back rudely;
argue;
smile condescendingly at others' words;
use elegant Chinese expressions;
boast;
avoid speaking directly;
speak with a knowing air;
jump from topic to topic;
use fancy words;
speak of past events that cannot be changed;
speak like a pedant;
avoid direct questions;
speak ill of others;
speak grandly of enlightenment;
carry on while drunk;
speak in an obnoxious manner;
yell at children;
make up fantastic stories;
speak while angry;
drop names;
ignore the people to whom you are speaking;
speak sanctimoniously of Gods and Buddhas;
use sugary speech;
use flattering speech;
speak of things of which you have no
    knowledge;
monopolize the conversation;
talk about others behind their backs;
speak with conceit;
bad-mouth others;
chant prayers ostentatiously;
complain about the amount of alms;
give long-winded sermons;

speak affectedly like an artist;
speak affectedly like a tea master.

Offer incense and flowers to the Buddha;
Plant trees and flowers, clean and water
  the garden;
Regularly use moxibustion for the legs;
Avoid oily fish;
Select light fare and avoid greasy food;
Do not oversleep;
Do not overeat;
Do not take too long an afternoon nap;
Do not exhaust yourself;
Do not be neglectful;
Do not speak when you have nothing to say;
Do not hide anything in your heart;
Always drink saké warm;
Shave your head;
Trim your nails;
Rinse your mouth and use a toothpick;
Take a bath;
Keep your voice clear.

The *I-Ching* states:
Happiness lies in the proper blend of:
  hot–cold
  good–bad
  black–white
  beautiful–ugly
  large–small
  wisdom–foolishness
  long–short
  brightness–darkness
  high–low
  partial–whole
  relaxation–quickness
  increase–decrease

purity–filth
slow–fast.

Ryōkan was forever leaving things behind. A number of letters to his friends survive, filled with sketches of articles he had misplaced and asking them if they had seen the objects in question. Sometimes he would beg at the same house twice on the same day, having forgotten his earlier visit, and be scolded by the mistress of the house for being greedy. Here is another list he made:

(1) Things to take along
Cotton cap, towel, tissue, paper, fan, coins, ball, marbles.

(2) Necessities
Bamboo hat, leggings, gloves, belt, staff, short surplice.

(3) For pilgrimages
Clothes, straw raincoat, bowl, bag.

Be sure to read this before going out or else you will have trouble!

As he entered his sixties, Ryōkan had a harder time getting around, so in 1816 he moved to another hermitage next to Otogo Shrine, at the base of Mount Kūgami. When he left Gogō-an, Ryōkan composed this poem:

On the slope of
Kūgami,
In the mountain shade
How many years
Was this hut my home?
Now it is time
To leave it empty—
My memory will fade

Gogō-an.
This is a replica built on the site of Ryōkan's hermitage on Mount Kūgami earlier this century.

The interior of Gogō-an.
Visible is a statue of Ryōkan in the alcove and the Buddhist altar next to it.

Like summer grasses.
Back and forth
I paced around it
And then walked away
Until the hut disappeared
Among the trees.
As I walk, I keep
Looking back after each bend,
Looking back at that place.

Ryōkan's life at Otogo Shrine was much like that at Gogō-an, the light mixing with the dark:

In Otogo Forest beneath Mount Kūgami
You'll find the tiny hut where I pass my days.
Still no temples or villas for me!
I'd rather live with the fresh breezes and the
    bright moon,

Playing with the village children or making
   poems.
If you ask about me, you'll probably say,
"What is that foolish monk doing now?"

An old infirm man of sixty years
Living next to a shrine apart from the village.
Midnight—the heavy rain violently pounds
   the rocks;
Beneath the window, a solitary light flickers.

As a boy, I studied the Chinese classics
   but could not master them;
As a youth, I practiced Zen but failed to
   transmit it.
Now living next door to a shrine,
Half Shintō priest, half Buddhist monk.

Ryōkan was finally obliged to leave his hermitage at Otogo
Shrine, too:

In a dilapidated three-room hut
I've grown old and tired;
This winter cold is the
Worst I've suffered through.
I sip thin gruel waiting for the
Freezing night to pass.
Can I last until spring finally arrives?
Unable to beg for rice,
How will I survive the chill?
Even meditation helps no longer;
Nothing left to do but compose poems
In memory of deceased friends.

In 1826, when he was sixty-eight, Ryōkan left Otogo Shrine
and went to live with the Kimura family in Shimazaki Village.
He was given a little building at the back of the property, but it

did not really suit him. He compared himself to the caged birds the Kimura family kept:

> Now and then
> You must long for the
> Freedom of the deep woods—
> I, too, cherish
> Such thoughts.

Ryōkan made one last visit to Gogō-an:

> I took my staff and slowly made my way
> Up to the hut where I spent so many years.
> The walls had crumbled, and it now sheltered
>   foxes and rabbits.
> The well by the bamboo grove was dry,
> And thick cobwebs covered the window where I
>   once read by moonlight.
> The steps were overrun with wild weeds,
> And a lone cricket sang in the bitter cold.
> I walked about fitfully, unable to tear myself
>   away
> As the sun set sadly.

On a happier note, it was during his stay at the Kimura residence that the seventy-year-old Ryōkan met and fell in love with the beautiful young nun Teishin (1798–1872). Although it evidently remained a platonic relationship, the bonds of love between them were as deep as those between Ikkyū and Lady Mori. After Teishin first met Ryōkan she wrote this poem:

> Was it really you
> I saw,
> Or is this joy
> I still feel
> Only a dream?

Ryōkan's reply was:

> In this dream world
> We doze
> And talk of dreams—
> Dream, dream on,
> As much as you wish.

There was also this exchange:

> Here with you
> I could remain
> For countless days and years,
> Silent as the bright moon
> We gazed at together.
> (Teishin)

> If your heart
> Remains unchanged,
> We will be bound as tightly
> As an endless vine
> For ages and ages.
> (Ryōkan)

When Teishin failed to visit Ryōkan, he sent her this plaintive verse:

> Have you forgotten me
> Or lost the path here?
> Now I wait for you
> All day, every day.
> But you do not appear.

Teishin wrote back complaining that her involvement with worldly affairs kept her away:

> The moon, I'm sure,

Is shining brightly
High above the mountains,
But gloomy clouds
Shroud the peak in darkness.

Ryōkan sent back this advice:

You must rise above
The gloomy clouds
Covering the mountaintop.
Otherwise, how will you
Ever see the brightness?

Snowed in all winter, Teishin was not able to visit Ryōkan until the spring thaw. When he saw her, Ryōkan exclaimed:

In all of heaven and earth,
There is nothing
More precious
Than a visit from you
On the first day of spring.

Because of his black robe and sunburned complexion, Ryōkan was nicknamed "Crow" by Teishin and their friends. (In the Far East, the crow is a symbol of eternal love.) Highly pleased, Ryōkan came up with this verse:

Free as a bird
To go wherever I please,
From tomorrow
I will take the name "Crow"
Given to me by my friends.

Teishin added at once:

When a mountain crow
Flies to his home,

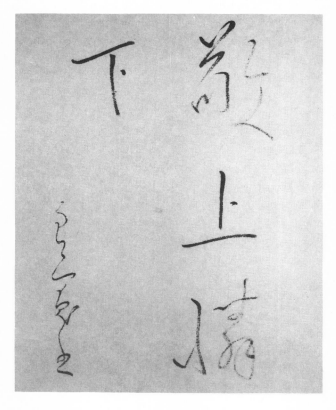

Ryōkan's Motto: "Respect your elders and be considerate of your juniors." (Kimura Collection, Japan)
This was brushed in the last year of Ryōkan's life.

Shouldn't he take along
His soft-winged
Little darling?

Ryōkan replied with a smile:

I'd love to take
You anywhere
I go,
But won't people suspect us
Of being lovebirds?

For the rest of Ryōkan's life they were together often, composing poems, discussing literature and religion, and walking through the neighboring villages and fields.

Chanting old poems,
Making our own verses,
Playing *temari*
Together in the fields—
Two people, one heart.

The breeze is fresh,
The moon so bright—
Together
Let's dance till dawn
As a farewell to my old age.

In the winter of 1830, Ryōkan's health failed completely. Stricken with terrible diarrhea, Ryōkan used poetry to complain:

It is an
Easy condition
To talk about,
But these runny bowels
Are killing me!

His physical decline was rapid, and when Teishin rushed to his deathbed Ryōkan declared his love for her:

> "When, when?" I sighed.
> The one I longed for
> Has finally come;
> With her now,
> I have all that I need.

She replied:

> We monastics are said
> To overcome the realm
> Of life and death—
> Yet I cannot bear the
> Sorrow of our parting.

Ryōkan answered quietly:

> Everywhere you look
> The crimson leaves
> Scatter—
> One by one,
> Front and back.

Ryōkan passed away early in the morning of January 6, 1831. His funeral, jointly officiated by priests from all the main Buddhist denominations, was attended by everyone in the village and the surrounding neighborhood.

> What will remain as my legacy?
> Flowers in the spring,
> The cuckoo in summer,
> And the crimson leaves
> Of autumn.

FURTHER READING

IKKYŪ

Primary sources of information on Ikkyū are:

Andō Hideo. *Ikkyū* (Tales of Ikkyū). Tokyo: Suzuki Shuppan, 1985.

Hirano, S., ed. *Ikkyū Oshō nenpū no kenkyū* (Studies on the Chronicles of Ikkyū's Life). Kyoto: Zen Bunka Kenkyū-jo, 1977.

Katō Shūichi, and Yanagida Seizan. *Nihon no Zen goroku: Ikkyū* (Zen Texts of Japan: Ikkyū). Tokyo: Kōdansha, 1977.

Mori Taikyō, ed. *Ikkyū Oshō zenshū* (The Complete Works of Ikkyū). Tokyo: Kōyū-an, 1913.

In English, see:

Arntzen, Sonya. *Ikkyū and the Crazy Cloud Anthology.* Tokyo: University of Tokyo Press, 1988.

Covell, Jon, and Yamada Sōbin. *Zen's Core: Ikkyū's Freedom.* Seoul: Hollym International, 1980.

———. *Zen at Daitoku-ji.* Tokyo: Kodansha International, 1974.

Fowkes, C. *The Pillow Book.* London: Hamlyn Publishing Group, 1988.

Sanford, J. H. *Zen-Man Ikkyū.* Chico, California: Scholar's Press, 1981.

HAKUIN

The main sources in Japanese for Hakuin's life are:

Hakuin Oshō Zenshū Hensan Kai, ed. *Hakuin Oshō zenshū* (The Complete Works of Hakuin). 8 vols. Tokyo: Ryūginsha, 1934–35.
Katō Shōshun. *Hakuin Oshō nenpū* (Annotated Biography of Hakuin). Kyoto: Shibunkaku, 1985.
Rikukawa Taiun. *Kōshō: Hakuin Oshō shōden* (The Complete Biography of Hakuin). Tokyo: Sankibō Busshōrin, 1963.

In English, see:

Tanahashi, Kazuaki. *Penetrating Laughter: Hakuin's Zen and Art.* Woodstock, New York: The Overlook Press, 1984.
Shaw, R. D. M. *The Embossed Tea Kettle.* London: George Allen & Unwin, 1963.
Yampolsky, Philip B. *The Zen Master Hakuin.* New York: Columbia University Press, 1971.

RYŌKAN

In Japanese, the best source of information on Ryōkan is:

Tōgō Toyohara. *Ryōkan zenshū* (The Complete Works of Ryōkan). 2 vols. Tokyo: Sōgensha, 1959.

Also good is:

Andō Hideo. *Ryōkan* (Tales of Ryōkan). Tokyo: Suzuki Shuppan, 1986.

In English, see:

Stevens, John. *One Robe, One Bowl: The Zen Poetry of Ryōkan.* Tokyo: John Weatherhill, 1977.
Watson, Burton. *Ryōkan: Zen Monk-Poet of Japan.* New York: Columbia University Press, 1981.
Yuasa, Nobuyuki. *The Zen Poems of Ryōkan.* Princeton, New Jersey: Princeton University Press, 1981.

GENERAL

Addiss, Stephen. *The Art of Zen.* New York: Harry N. Abrams, 1989.

Besserman, P., and Steger, M. *Crazy Clouds: Zen Radicals, Rebels and Reformers.* Boston: Shambhala Publications, 1991.

Stevens, John. *Lust for Enlightenment: Buddhism and Sex.* Boston: Shambhala Publications, 1990.

————. *Sacred Calligraphy of the East.* Boston: Shambhala Publications, 1988.

————. *Zenga: Brushstrokes of Enlightenment.* New Orleans: New Orleans Museum of Art, 1990.

DISCOVER JAPAN, VOLS. 1 AND 2
Words, Customs, and Concepts

The Japan Culture Institute

Essays and photographs illuminate 200 ideas and customs of Japan.

THE UNFETTERED MIND
Writings of the Zen Master to the Sword Master

Takuan Sōhō / Translated by William Scott Wilson

Philosophy as useful to today's corporate warriors as it was to seventeenth century samurai.

THE JAPANESE THROUGH AMERICAN EYES

Sheila K. Johnson

"Cogent...as skeptical of James Clavell's *Shogun* as it is of William Ouchi's *Theory Z*."—*Publisher's Weekly*

Available only in Japan.

BEYOND NATIONAL BORDERS
Reflections on Japan and the World

Kenichi Ohmae

"[Ohmae is Japan's] only management guru."—*Financial Times*

Available only in Japan.

THE COMPACT CULTURE
The Japanese Tradition of "Smaller is Better"

O-Young Lee / Translated by Robert N. Huey

A long history of skillfully reducing things and concepts to their essentials reveals the essence of the Japanese character and, in part, accounts for Japan's business success.

THE HIDDEN ORDER
Tokyo through the Twentieth Century

Yoshinobu Ashihara

"Mr. Ashihara shows how, without anybody planning it, Japanese architecture has come to express the vitality of Japanese life."
—*Daniel J. Boorstin*

THE ANATOMY OF SELF
The Individual Versus Society
Takeo Doi / Translated by Mark A. Harbison
"An excellent book."
—*Frank A. Johnson, M.D., University of California, San Francisco*

HOME, SWEET TOKYO
Life in a Weird and Wonderful City
Rick Kennedy
Wry commentaries reveal the charm and humor behind Tokyo's "solemn wackiness."

JAPAN'S LONGEST DAY
The Pacific War Research Society
A detailed account of the day before Japan surrendered.

WORDS IN CONTEXT
A Japanese Perspective on Language and Culture
Takao Suzuki / Translated by Akira Miura
Explores the complex relationship between language and culture.

JAPANESE RELIGION
A Survey by the Agency for Cultural Affairs
Edited by Ichirō Hori
A clear and factual introduction to Japanese Religion.

MIRROR, SWORD, AND JEWEL
The Geometry of Japanese Life
Kurt Singer
"This glimpse of Japanese culture is totally engrossing."
—*Publisher's Weekly*

APPRECIATIONS OF JAPANESE CULTURE
Donald Keene
A glimpse at the complexities that interact to form the Japanese character.